Mama Was My Teacher

Mama

Mama Was My Teacher

Growing Up In A Small Southern Town

Dozier C. Cade

iUniverse, Inc.

New York Lincoln Shanghai

Mama Was My Teacher
Growing Up In A Small Southern Town

iUniverse, Inc.

For information address:
iUniverse, Inc.
2021 Pine Lake Road, Suite 100
Lincoln, NE 68512
www.iuniverse.com

ISBN: 0-595-30741-8

Printed in the United States of America

To my wonderful wife Kay and my dear sister Ruth

Men are what their mothers made them.

—Ralph Waldo Emerson

*   *   *

I have had playmates, I have had companions,
In my days of childhood, in my joyful school-days,
All, all are gone, the old familiar faces.

—Charles Lamb

CONTENTS

LIST OF ILLUSTRATIONS

FOREWORD

I was born in the lovely little town of Eufaula in southeast Alabama, then separated from Georgia by the Chattahoochee River and now by Lake Eufaula. Eufaula is about 45 miles from Columbus, Georgia on the north and about 60 miles from Dothan, Alabama on the south. Panama City, Florida, with its white sandy beaches, beckons only 140 miles away.

Eufaula was, and still is, a pretty place and a great place to grow up in. Stately old well-kept homes, beautiful flowers, towering trees, wide streets, nice genteel people. I wouldn't take anything for being born into a low-income family and having to work for things I got instead of having them handed to me as many youngsters do today. I learned the value of a penny, much less a dollar, and what I learned lives with me today.

We had good schools and loving, caring teachers. Life was simple but full of warm, happy days and childhood pleasures. We never got bored. There was so much to do and so little time during the day to do it. Night always came far too quickly.

Our family of seven didn't have much, but we had lots of love and a loving mother and a caring father, neither of whom had much formal education. There were older brother Jimmy and older sister Mildred, and younger sister Ruth and younger brother Horace. All are dead now except me and Ruth who still lives in Eufaula and whom I love dearly.

I had many boyhood friends and most of them are now dead too, except Eufaula's noted historian, Robert Flewellen, who still lives in Eufaula and who loves that town probably more than I do—and that's saying a lot.

When people ask me where I'm from, I always say Eufaula. When they ask me where I live, I say Hilton Head Island. I'll always be "from" Eufaula. I've been away from Eufaula in a sense since I left home for the University of Alabama in 1935.

In another sense I've never left Eufaula. Over the years I went there every chance I got, no matter how far away I lived at the time, and I still go there every time I can. Such times, unfortunately, are getting farther and farther apart.

But my heart is still there, and always will be.

CHAPTER 1

Love Was Her Name, Love Was Her Life

My Mama was a beautiful Irish lady. Dark black hair until it turned snowy, silky white. Ruddy, clear complexion.

Her name was Love Ellis, and when she was only 18 she left her home and family in Enterprise, Alabama for Eufaula, Alabama and became Love Ellis Cade on St Patrick's Day in 1907.

No one could have had a more fitting name. Love was her life. She loved people. She loved making people feel good. She loved making people happy. Above all, she loved her family of husband, three boys and two girls. She was Love personified.

When she died of a heart attack at age 70, I'm sure she went to that place where Love was born. I just wish I could have told her I loved her one more time before she died.

Many times Mama said to me, "Little Dozier, I want to tell you something." She called me Little Dozier because Daddy was still Big Dozier years later when I became taller than he was. When she started her talks with me like that, I knew I should listen carefully because I was about to learn some important truth I would want to remember. So one day she said:

"Little Dozier, if every day you do something nice for somebody, say something nice to them, do something to help them in some way, say something that will make them feel better about themselves, pay them some compliment, just do

1

anything that will make them happy, even for just a minute, then your life will have been worth living."

I never forgot what Mama said. Every day of my life I've tried to do what she told me to and my own life has been happier as a result.

Mama would always say something nice about somebody if somebody else said something bad about that person. Like, "Yes, that may be true, but she sure does bake good cakes." Or, "Yes, but he always pays his bills on time."

George Eliot must have had somebody like Mama in mind when she wrote:

> If you sit down at set of sun
> And count the acts that you have done,
> And, counting, find
> One self-denying deed, one word
> That eased the heart of him who heard,
> One glance most kind
> That fell like sunshine where it went,
> Then you may count that day well spent.
> But if, through all the livelong day,
> You've cheered no heart, by yea or nay,
> If, through it all
> You've nothing done that you can trace
> That brought the sunshine to one face,
> No act most small
> That helped some soul and nothing cost,
> Then count that day as worse than lost.

This version of Mary Davis Reed's "One Year to Live" echoes Mama's philosophy of life, which I have adopted as my own:

> If I had but a year to live,
> A year to help, a year to give,
> A year to love, a year to bless,
> A year of better things to stress,
> A year to sing, a year to smile,
> To brighten earth a little while,
> I think that I would spend each day
> In just the very self-same way
> As I do now. For I must be
> Prepared to meet eternity.
> So if I have a year to live,

Or just a day in which to give
A pleasant smile, a helping hand,
A heart that tries to understand
A fellow-creature when in need,
'Tis one with me, I take no heed,
But try to live each day I can,
Hoping to help my fellow man.

CHAPTER 2

If Anything's Worth Doing, It's Worth Doing Right

With five children in the house, and so much to do to keep things going, we all had chores to do. Equal employment opportunity was available in our household.

One of my jobs was sweeping the front yard every day. By front yard, I don't mean a yard with grass, well-pruned shrubs and beautiful and expensive flowering plants. We did have flowers planted here and there. I mean a dirt yard, which constantly was bombarded with acorns, countless tree twigs and bird droppings, added to bits of broken glass and assorted minutiae.

What I'm saying is, it wasn't easy to keep that big yard clean, especially when you didn't have a real broom or rake to use.

I used something like a broom made of either green or dead tree branches tied together with heavy brown string. It wasn't easy to sweep our yard but I persevered, even if it cost me precious playtime or marble-shooting time.

I knew I had to do a good job because I couldn't do anything else until Mama inspected and passed my sweeping. Mama's inspections would make an Army sergeant realize he needed to go to Inspection School.

One day I was in a hurry to dig some worms and go fishing, so, as the saying goes, I gave the yard "a lick and a promise." Mama came out to look things over.

I could tell by her face, which was ruddier than usual, she didn't like what she saw.

"Little Dozier," she began, "I want to tell you something. If something is worth doing, it's worth doing right. I want you to remember that the rest of your life, whatever you do. Now clean that yard. THEN you can go fishing."

I felt ashamed, but I'm glad it happened. All my life I've always tried to do a good job, whatever I did. So I'm called a perfectionist. If you had had a Mama like mine, you'd be one, too.

When boys got together and argued about something and one of the boys said, "My Mama said so-and-so," that ended the argument. We all knew whatever our mamas said was true. No boy would dare contradict what somebody else's mama said. Mamas were sacrosanct in those days. It's a pity they still aren't.

One of the boys at school was named Clara. His mama died when he was born and his daddy named him after his mama. I think everybody liked Clara more for that reason. We never teased him about his name. Woe be to any boy who did. He soon found out why he shouldn't—the hard way.

CHAPTER 3

Mama Had A Language Of Her Own

I remember the things Mama told me because they were simple truths. She got right to the point, telling it like it was. No flowery language. Just plain Mama. Her little talks have stayed with me to this very minute, and have helped change my life for the better. Today I am who I am mainly because of what Mama taught me. She and her simple words of wisdom long ago still seem near to me.

Most of all, I learned from Mama that I didn't know it all, that I will always have a lot to learn, that I will never stop learning until the day I die.

Mama brought me down to earth when I got too high and mighty, or bragged on myself for what I knew or for something I did. Sometimes I felt my oats and got a little smart-alecky. All Mama had to say was, "Little Dozier, you're honey. But the bees don't know it." I got the point.

She had another expression to refer to a know-it-all: "Why he's (she's) a regular Jessie's puppy." Figure that one out.

Sometimes when I got angry with somebody or got into an argument, I used intemperate language. One day after such an outburst which Mama heard, she said to me, "Little Dozier, always remember this. You can catch more bees with honey than you can with vinegar."

That advice has come in handy for me many times when I wanted something from somebody or tried to persuade somebody to see things my way.

I never knew where Mama's favorite expression came from, but I knew what it meant, even if it's not a dictionary word. When she did or said something that embarrassed her, or that she knew she shouldn't have done or said, she would say: "I sure was chaud about that."

I don't even know how to spell the word, but it sounded like c-h-a-w-e-d or c-h-a-u-d. Maybe it came from Mama's Gaelic ancestral memory. Mama is the only person I ever heard use the word. I still use it sometimes. Nobody knows what I'm talking about except my wife Kay who has heard the story. Perhaps we should put the word in the dictionary. It's simpler and shorter than "chagrined," which is what Mama probably meant.

A French word "chaud" means hot or warm. Maybe Mama meant she was in hot water.

Mama often used another word, "miration." If you made a big-to-do about something she would say, "Well, you don't have to make such a miration about it." The word was probably a derivation of admiration. I knew what she meant: "Calm down. Cool it. That's enough."

Sometimes when Mama would speak to somebody, or ask somebody a question, and that person said nothing or made no answer, Mama would say: "Why she (or he) didn't even say pea turkey." I have no idea where she got that expression. I just knew it meant the person didn't say anything.

CHAPTER 4

Depression Days

We were a family with a low income, although we always had plenty to eat, enough clothes to wear and lots of love around us. During the Depression, Daddy lost what little money he had—including all his savings—in the Commercial National Bank when it closed in 1931.

He never put another penny in a bank, so he never wrote another check. Each month he would cash his pay-check, gather up all his bills, take them to the various creditors, get paid-up receipts, and keep them on a spike at home.

Because of the Depression, it was hard for town officials in Eufaula to pay the school teachers enough. So parents had to supplement teachers' salaries by paying tuition. Some families couldn't afford to pay it, and with five children in school, we were one of them. Daddy had to attest to his inability to pay by signing an oath to that effect. I know it hurt Daddy. It did us.

At the beginning of the school year, we had to bring certificates to school signifying we either had paid the tuition or weren't able to do so. People who paid brought pale-yellow certificates, those who didn't brought red ones. Or it may have been the other way around. Memory not only dims but also reverses things sometimes.

Fortunately we had a home-room teacher, "Miss Annie" Ballowe, who was wise and caring, so she told the class: "Now children, you are supposed to bring your certificates to school tomorrow. Now all of you must put them in sealed envelopes before you hand them in. I will take no certificates unless you do."

Bless her heart, I still love her dearly, and always will, though she left me and her other "children" a long time ago. Every time I came home after graduation I went to see her.

I had many school friends—some richer, some poorer, some about like us. It did bother me that other children had more money than we did and could hand in paid certificates, even though in "Miss Annie's" class you couldn't tell who handed in red or who brought yellow. Most kids knew or suspected, though, and talked with each other about who probably brought which color.

On one certificate day I came home after school, went to my room and lay down on the bed. I usually started studying when I came home so I could listen to the radio at night. Mama came into the room.

"Little Dozier, why aren't you studying? Aren't you feeling well?"

I told her what was on my mind. She listened, then put her arms around me.

"Little Dozier, I want to tell you something. I want you to remember this one thing, if you don't remember anything else. Nobody is better than you are. Now you aren't any better than anybody else, but nobody is better than you. The good Lord made us all, and he loves us all just the same, and nobody is better than anybody else."

As a newspaperman, I've rubbed shoulders with and been on close terms with the high and the mighty as well as the low and the unmighty, and I've never been impressed by the rich and famous nor looked down on the poor and lowly. Certainly I've never been impressed with myself.

Not after what you told me one September afternoon after school, Mama, when I was lying on my bed and feeling blue about that red certificate.

CHAPTER 5

Girls

When I was 14, and little girls I had known and played with were big girls now and a whole lot different, I started having real dates and not each-pay-your-own-way-and-buy-your-own-candy picture-show dates. I had kissed a few girls, but most of the kisses were brief pecks on the cheeks or lip touchings and pressings.

By then I was dating a girl regularly. You might call Edith my first sweetheart. Each Sunday night I would walk up to her house on Cherry Street and listen with her on the radio to the romantic music of Wayne King and his Orchestra. He was known as The Waltz King. I always got there early to get settled on the living-room sofa so I wouldn't miss any of his theme song, "The Waltz You Saved for Me."

Mama knew all this, so one day she said to me: "Little Dozier, you've started dating girls about now, haven't you?"

I started to be my sometimes smart-alecky self and answer, "No ma'm, I'm still dating boys."

But I knew this was serious business. She had that look and tone of voice. So I did what I usually do when girls were mentioned or I was around them.

I blushed and looked down.

"Little Dozier, I want to ask you something."

"Yes'm?"

"How do you like for boys to treat your sisters when they date them?"

"Well, uh, I'd like them to be nice to them, to treat them nice, not try to do bad things to them."

"All right. Just remember, every time you date a girl, you treat her like you would want a boy to treat your sister."

I always did just what Mama told me. I'm sure I wouldn't be married to my wonderful wife Kay today if I hadn't.

So I knew just what I should do when I had my first real kiss.

It was a beautiful, slightly cool, early Spring night. We were sitting on her front doorsteps and all of a sudden I had this funny feeling in my head and stomach, and I just had to do it

I put my arm around her and my eager mouth on those large, warm, velvety Betty-Grable-like lips and slowly pressed them—ever so gently, then a bit harder, then hard and persistently.

All of a sudden I had feelings all over I had never had before. I knew there was only one thing to do. I got up and ran all the way home.

Later, when I was a student at Northwestern University, I kissed the real Betty Grable at the Hotel Sherman in Chicago, where she was singing with her husband Harry James' band. Her lips were just as I described them above: "large, warm, velvety."

Some of my college housemates and I were taking a night off from our studies that Saturday night for some R & R—Rest and Recreation in Army lingo. We had a front-row table.

"I sure would like to kiss her," I sighed aloud.

My Utah roommate got up and walked to the bandstand. I saw him in earnest conversation with Miss Grable.

Pretty soon he came back with her.

"I hear a little old Southern boy wants to kiss me," she said teasingly. "I've always wanted to kiss a little old Southern boy. Would you like to kiss me?"

My face felt warm. I blushed, and looked down. As usual.

"Yes m'am, I sure would. That would be mighty nice."

"Stand up then."

"Yes'm."

Then she wrapped her cream-colored arms around me and, in a word or four, laid one on me. Sorta like the one described above, except less urgent, more gently and more abbreviated. But the effects were about the same.

This time I didn't run home. I just sat down. Real quick.

CHAPTER 6

Fishing And Bread Scraps

Mama liked to go fishing. She'd fish anywhere she could. Creeks, rivers, ponds. She especially liked to fish in ponds her friends owned, because she could stake out the best places to fish. If she went by herself she had to walk. When we boys got older and had cars, we could drive her anywhere she wanted to go.

One day when I was at home after the war I drove her to one of those private ponds. We got our bait from the worm bed in the back yard. The bed's black soil was covered with old rotten planks and watered daily. Coffee grounds and bread scraps were dumped on the bed to attract wigglers and those juicy, pink, segmented worms bream love.

"Now we've got to get home by 5:30," she told me. "I've got to get your Daddy's supper to him by 6."

Daddy was a Railway Express agent on the Central of Georgia Railroad running between Montgomery and Macon. He came through Eufaula in the late afternoon about 6 from Montgomery and again the next morning about 7 from Macon.

Mama always brought him his supper and breakfast, walking from Orange Street to and from the station when she didn't have a ride. The train didn't follow an exact time-table, and could come in the station up to 15 minutes earlier or later than scheduled.

"We can stay a little later this time than I usually can because you've got the car and I don't have to walk," she said.

"Yes'm," I said. "We'll leave in plenty of time. I'll get you there."

Well, the fishing was real good. Mama was having fits as she hauled in bream and catfish one after the other, about as fast as she could bait her hook.

"Boy, we've got a mess of fish. I don't know how I'll ever be able to clean 'em all."

Time passes quickly when you're catching fish. Pretty soon it was getting late.

"Mama, we'd better go. It's nearly 5 o'clock and you've got to fix Daddy's supper."

"No, I fixed it before I left. It's in a sack in the refrigerator. All I got to do is pick it up and we'll go."

"Yes'm, but we've got to leave real soon. It'll take us about 15 minutes to get home."

"I know. We'll make it. All I've got to do is pick up the sack."

My watch's hands sped to 5:25. "Mama, we've GOT to go. Now!"

It took us about 5 minutes to haul in the string of fish, quickly wind our lines on the long bamboo poles, get our poles through the open car windows, and stow our fishing gear in the car.

We walked in the house at 5:45. Just then the train whistle blew. Fifteen minutes early this time, of all times. The train wouldn't stay in the station long.

"My God!" Mama said. "We're gonna miss your Daddy's train and he won't get his supper!"

Mama used earthy language on occasions, but she was a religious person and meant no disrespect to God.

She rushed to the refrigerator, grabbed a sack and yelled: "Let's go!"

We got to the station just as the train was pulling out. Mama threw the sack into the Express car.

The next morning Mama took Daddy's breakfast to him as usual. This time she was early.

Daddy was grinning as the train rolled to a stop.

"Cade," he said (they sometimes called each other Cade for no reason I know of), "them sure was good bread scraps you brought me for supper last night."

"My God!" Mama said. "I must have picked up the wrong bag!"

When she made sandwiches, Mama usually put the bread crusts in a sack and kept them in the refrigerator. Sometimes she toasted them in the oven to go with soup, or put them on the bait bed to add to the "mix" to produce plumper and juicier worms.

When she got back home, she found Daddy's night-before supper in another sack in the refrigerator.

Mama was chaud, to put it mildly. Daddy never let her forget it. He liked to tease her any chance he got.

"What're we having for supper tonight, Cade? Some more of them good bread scraps?"

Mama didn't quite know how to take Daddy's teasing, and as I've said, she used pretty earthy language, so I won't say what she told Daddy to do with those bread scraps.

One night Mama and some of her neighbor friends were sitting in rocking chairs on the front porch shelling peas and butterbeans and snapping string beans and talking about this and that, all the while rocking and jawing.

Mama did love to talk Daddy didn't have much to say. He didn't have a chance to. They called it making conversation. Some might call it gossiping. It was one way of getting together socially and at the same time relieving the tedium and boredom of their work.

Daddy was sitting in the porch swing. I was a curious listener on the front steps.

Unbelievably there was a lull in the conversation. All you could hear were bean-snapping, and peas and butterbeans falling in the aluminum pots.

Daddy cleared his throat cough-like.

"Cade, I want to ask you something. Are you sure everything you're saying is the truth?"

If Daddy had gone where Mama told him to, he sure would have been hot.

Daddy was a Democrat all his life. He never voted Republican, but he almost did once. He told me he had decided to vote for Eisenhower for President, but when he got into the polling booth and started to write Eisenhower on the ballot, his right hand started trembling and he just couldn't do it.

However, he did like Norman Thomas, the highly respected perennial Presidential candidate of the Socialist Party. "I would vote for him if he was a Democrat," Daddy told me.

By coincidence, my wife and I moved into our present apartment only a few doors down the hall from Evan Thomas, Norman's son. Evan's widow Anne still lives there. A determined Democrat like my Daddy.

Her son, named for his father, is assistant managing editor and lead writer of Newsweek, a best-selling author, and a frequent participant on national television programs and talk shows.

Daddy looked a lot like the late President Harry Truman. He wore the same kind of hat President Truman did, and also had similar facial features, glasses and all.

One time when Mama and Daddy were visiting us while I was teaching at Northwestern I took them to the Brookfield Zoo in nearby Chicago. While Mama and I were animal-looking, Daddy decided to take a rest on one of the zoo's benches. People came up to him for autographs, thinking he was Truman.

For many years Daddy kept a journal of memorable events, local and elsewhere. He recorded illnesses, accidents, deaths, births, marriages, trips, floods, storms, earthquakes, wars, news events, elections, weather and what have you. He noted them in a long gray ledger.

As Daddy got older, he developed some of the infirmities of aging but still walked around town every day until he could no longer do so, and ended his days in 1975 at age 91 in a Eufaula nursing home.

During his walks and at other times, people would ask Daddy how he felt. Whether he felt good or bad, he would always say, "Jes' right." He said it so often people even began to call him "Jes' Right."

One time during a visit to Montgomery someone from Eufaula sent Daddy a postcard addressed only "Just Right, Eufaula, Alabama." The postman delivered it to him.

I asked Daddy why he always told people he was feeling that way when sometimes he felt really bad.

"Dozier," he said, "when people ask you how you're feeling they don't really want to know all the details of your ailments. They're just being polite and passing the time of day. So I tell them, 'Jes' right'."

Some of Daddy's friends and relatives sometimes called him "Uncle Bud." I don't know why, except maybe it was because of a little jingle he often recited to his children and grandchildren: "Uncle Bud and Aunt Jane went chinquapin huntin', Aunt Jane fell down and Uncle Bud seen...."

I won't repeat the ending. You can imagine.

Another little rhyme he used to recite to me when I was a boy:

> Jaybird sittin' on a hick'ry lim',
> He looked at me and I looked at him,
> I picked up a rock and I hit him on the chin,
> And he said, "Little boy, don't you do that ag'in."

CHAPTER 7

Cholesterol, Where Art Thou?...In Mama's Kitchen

Mama loved to cook. The kitchen was her castle. Her high stool was her throne. Her cooking was constant. Three meals a day for seven people.

A full breakfast from among fried, scrambled or boiled eggs, brains and eggs, plain grits, cheese grits, fatback, bacon, link or patty sausage, ripe or green tomatoes fried in bacon grease, buttermilk biscuits, egg gravy, waffles, pancakes, cane syrup, home-made butter, jellies and preserves, crisp fried corn meal patties, cocoa or Maxwell House coffee. Maybe even salt mackerel on Saturday. I loved Mama's fig preserves. The figs came from a tree in the back yard. Sometimes she made fig newtons from them.

Incidentally, some famous non-Southern grits eaters were Union General Ulysses S. Grant, Franklin D. Roosevelt and Captain John Smith. Only Yankees eat grits with butter, sugar and milk. They must think it's Southern cream of wheat.

We had a full dinner for what most people now call lunch. Mama would select her menu from among these foods:

A meat (pork chops, ham, fried or baked chicken, fried catfish), several vegetables cooked with ham hock, bacon grease or butter—corn, turnips, turnip greens, rutabagas, collards, cabbage, squash, crowder peas, field peas, black-eyed peas, butter beans, string beans, buttery boiled onions—creamed carrots, okra, rice, creamed or boiled potatoes, sliced tomatoes, home-made Wesson Oil and lemon mayonnaise, corn bread (not the sweet kind you get today that tastes like cake) or corn muffins, buttered yeast rolls.

Candied yams, baked sweet potatoes, a crusted marshmallow-covered sweet potato souffle', macaroni and cheese, spaghetti, potato salad, peach pickles, watermelon rind pickles, cucumber bread-and-butter pickles, pickle relish, tomato relish, watermelon, cantaloupe or musk melon, various kinds of cakes and pies—pecan, sweet potato, chocolate, coconut, lemon meringue—bread pudding, banana pudding, Tetley's ice tea, sweet milk, buttermilk.

Always fried chicken, or baked chicken with corn bread dressing, and candied yams or sweet potato casserole on Sundays. What was left over from dinner we had for supper.

Some more of Mama's Southern delicacies:

Ambrosia, just orange slices and coconut, always served at Christmas, usually with a red cherry on top; red-eye gravy, made by adding a little water or coffee to the residue left in the frying pan when ham is fried, goes well with grits; hominy, which is dried whole corn kernels boiled with lye to loosen the husk, then rinsed and dried; hushpuppies, deep-fried corn meal nuggets with onions, self-rising flour and a tad of sugar added, good with fried catfish and fried shrimp.

Crackling bread, which is corn bread embellished with crispy "cracklings," what's left over when hog fat is cooked down into lard, good with butter and syrup; clabber, a gelatinous goop resulting from sour sweet milk, good with corn bread and a bit of sugar, eaten with a spoon; pot likker, the liquid that's left over after turnip greens are cooked for a long time, flavored with pork grease, good with corn bread, corn muffins or corn dumplings.

Years later when I worked for the Atlanta Journal, I used to go to lunch at Emile's, a fancy French restaurant, with Ralph McGill, editor of the Atlanta Constitution. Although it obviously wasn't on the menu, the chef prepared a special lunch for Mr. McGill, a native Tennesseean. It consisted of turnip greens, black-eyed peas with pepper sauce, buttermilk, corn bread or corn muffins, and pot likker, which he used for his soup du jour.

He took me along because I liked the same, and was one of the few people he knew who appreciated good food. He crumbled his corn bread or corn muffins in his bowl of pot likker. I dunked mine. It's a matter of Southern choice. Pot likker with round corn dumplings in it looks like matzos ball soup.

Incidentally, for people who live above The Line, pot likker won't make you drunk. Neither will cotton gin.

Notice how much food made from corn we ate. In their delightful book, "1001 Things Everyone Should Know About the South," authors John Shelton Reed and Dale Volberg Reed pointed out that corn turns up throughout

Southern cooking. "This was noted in the 1860s by visiting Union soldiers, who called the South the 'corn-fed-racy'", they wrote.

So you see, cholesterol was not in the Cade dictionary those days. It was in Mama's kitchen.

Daddy sat at one end of the table, Mama at the other, nearest the kitchen. She was up and down most of the meals. Daddy always said the blessing, the same one every meal, for years on end: "The Lord make us thankful for this food and all thy many blessings. Amen." Was there really any need to say anything more? I still say the same blessing.

When the platters were passed around the table, Daddy always got the first serving, Mama the last. When we had fried chicken, we all wanted the pulley-bone so we could break it in two and make a wish. Mama got the last pick. I never did think that was fair because she did the cooking.

She invariably picked the back, which was one of the last pieces left. That had the least meat on it and a protuberance on the rear. Mama called it the parson's nose or the part of the chicken that went over the fence last. She claimed that was the tastiest part of the chicken. I liked the gizzard best myself. Drumstick second.

Mama told us we should eat everything on our plates. "Don't take any more than you want and eat everything you take. If you want more, you can have it. But don't leave anything on your plate. Think of the poor starving Armenians."

I didn't know who the poor starving Armenians were, but I figured they were poor hungry people off somewhere in the world, and that if I didn't eat everything on my plate they would starve.

If Mama said so, it was true. I never could figure out, though, how I could get what was left on my plate to the poor starving Armenians, but I didn't have the nerve to tell Mama that. I did learn later about the big famines in Armenia, especially the one in 1915, two years before I was born.

We had supper early so we could eat, get the table cleared and the dishes done so we could sit around the oval-shaped Atwater Kent radio at 6 o'clock to hear the Amos 'n Andy show, featuring squeaky-voiced Amos, gravel-voiced Andy, the con-guy Kingfish, and the flapper Madame Queen, the object of affection by both Andy and the Kingfish.

Later on in the night I liked to hear "The Shadow," then went to bed and pulled the covers over my head, the sepulchral voice "The Shadow knows" still whispering in my ears. Coincidentally, I wound up living in our present apartment a few doors away from the man who produced that show. He turned out to be just a nice harmless man after all.

The Atwater Kent was our first radio operated by electricity. Our first radio was a small crystal set with headphones. You could barely hear the stations on it, but we got such far away places as KDKA Pittsburgh, WLW Cincinnati, KWKH (for the owner William K. Henderson) Shreveport, and a station in Del Rio, Texas whose call letters I can't remember.

But what magic it was at the time! Radio stations, and some television stations, still keep the W or the K in their call letters.

We grew or raised most of our food ourselves. We grew the vegetables in a garden behind the house. We dug the furrows for planting and cultivating by pushing two wooden handles attached to a pointed hoe and connected to a large metal wheel. It was hard going, but the garden was too small to use a mule-drawn hoe. Weeding the garden was literally a pain in the back.

We had a milk cow for our sweet milk, buttermilk, butter and cream. Sometimes the cow ate some bitterweeds and the milk tasted like—bitterweeds. We raised chickens for our eggs and to eat, and a passel of pigs for ham, pork, sausage, and grease to season the vegetables—when Mama didn't use butter or store-bought lard. Animal and chicken droppings were used for garden fertilizer.

Later, probably for health and sanitary reasons, the town fathers decreed no more cows and pigs in the town limits. They let the chickens be, thank goodness, but we had to buy our sweet milk and buttermilk, cream, butter, meat and fertilizer.

We missed, gladly, the early-morning milkings, especially during the winter. I learned early, after being tail-switched in the face several times, that cows don't like cold hands.

As I said, Mama loved to cook. Christmas time was her glory time. She baked 10 or 12 different kinds of cakes: chocolate, coconut, angel food, caramel, pound, lane, devil's food, fruit, Japanese fruit, white frosting, domino, lemon cheese and maybe one or two more I can't remember. I got to lick the spoons and scrape up the good stuff left over in the mixing bowls.

The cakes wouldn't sit there just to be looked at, though they were sights to behold. They were so pretty I hated to see them cut into. They tasted better warm, and you were lucky to get a warm piece just out of the oven.

By New Year's Day they were all gone, crumbs and all, what with drop-in company helping demolish them. I hated to see the drop-ins eat so much, so I would ask Mama not to cut their pieces so big so we would have more cake to eat ourselves.

Daddy kept a small bottle of whisky in the dining-room cabinet storage area where the cakes were. He said you never knew when a snake might crawl in and bite somebody and you'd need some snake-bite medicine.

One Christmas Day while the rest of the family were snoozing or plopped down in chairs or on sofas after the big meal, I got Daddy's "medicine bottle," poured some whisky in a saucer of milk, and sat it down in front of our old yellow cat. The cat started lapping the mixture of milk and likker, shook his head from side to side, blew out air and milk spray from his nose, and kept on lapping.

We had a fire in the fireplace, and that old cat tried to make it to the fire to lie down. When he tried to walk, his legs buckled up under him. His meowing sounded more like a guttural, drunken snarl: "Meowwwrrr." He finally crawled on his stomach to the fireplace, stretched out on his back with all four feet in the air, and went sound asleep.

He slept all afternoon, till supper-time. The rest of the family thought he might be sick from eating too much. I said I thought he was just tired from celebrating Christmas.

CHAPTER 8

Mama's Gonna Whip You!

I wasn't exactly the nicest kid on the block when I was growing up. I got my share of whippings, as we called them. It didn't matter what the instrument of torture was: a belt, a leather strap (we called it strop), a paddle, a switch, or whatever was handy at the time. It was still called a whipping.

Mama was the chief whipper. She usually used a switch. I hated switches. They hurt. They stung. They left red welts on your legs. But they were supposed to hurt. Otherwise you wouldn't be properly punished. I would much rather have been leather-stropped any day by Daddy than stung with a switch by Mama.

The strop was wider than a switch. It made more noise but didn't hurt as much. Daddy was away at work most of the time, or asleep in bed because of his day-and-night railroad job, so I usually got Mama's switch. I deserved more whippings than I got. They were great character builders.

Most of my whippings were family-related. I used to devil my younger sister Ruth, and she used to devil me, but I usually wound up getting the whipping, probably because I was older and I was a boy. Also it was easier to whip me. All Mama or Daddy had to do was catch me.

Horace was too bony to feel the whipping much. But Ruth had it best of all. She squatted down, put her hands behind her head, then bowed down and made such a small target it was hard to really whip her.

I got much of mine on the run. A switch had a long reach. Lots of times I crawled under the house. Mama either waited me out or I outlasted her and she gave up. Or had other things to do.

I didn't have much to do with my older brother Jimmy, not because I didn't love him. After all, he was a left-handed pitcher for Eufaula High and sang in the glee club. He was nine years older than I and too grown-up to have much to do with me.

My older sister Mildred was so sweet to me I never did anything untoward to her. She read to me, hugged me and kissed me a lot, unbuttoned my britches for me at school when I had to go to the toilet, and later sent me money when I went to college.

I never saw either of them get a whipping. They were past that stage when I was little.

My younger brother Horace used to tease me to provoke my baser nature. We slept in the same bed.

One morning after he had been tickling me under my chin I told him if he didn't stop he'd be sorry. He didn't stop. So I flexed my legs and shove-kicked him off the bed, through the window panes, through the window screen, into the garden, up against the scuppernong vines.

Fortunately for both of us, he wasn't hurt. Maybe his pride. He started crying, of course, and said I would get a whipping. I did, but it was worth it. He stopped teasing me.

Horace didn't cry when he was whipped. He just stood there and took it. He didn't make a sound. I think it sorta exasperated Mama and Daddy. Maybe he was braver than I. Or bonier. Or had a higher threshold of pain.

I wish Horace were here to tease me again, and Jimmy to ignore me, and Mildred to hug and kiss me….

One of my daily duties was to get fresh butter from a neighbor friend of the family. I would get Mama's best china saucer—she wouldn't think of using anything but her best china for other people to see—and take it to Mrs. Mainor's.

She used a long wooden spoon to dip the butter from freshly churned buttermilk, patted it into a round wooden mold, packed it in, smoothed it out, and dumped the perfectly round cake of butter onto the saucer—with a pretty leafy design imprinted on the butter by the mold.

I liked to play marbles for halves or for keeps, thinly disguised words to hide the fact that my playing was a form of gambling. We boys drew a large circle with a stick, put some peewees (small brownish clay marbles) and agate marbles (prettier and costlier larger glass ones) into the ring, knelt along the circumference of the circle, and used our agate shooters or steelies (steel ball bearings) to knock marbles out of the ring. We took turns, one shot at a time, and what we knocked out we kept.

Well, Mama didn't like gambling. She thought it was a sin. Unfortunately, sister Ruth knew I played that wicked game with some friends on my way to Mrs. Mainor's, and she used that knowledge to her best blackmail advantage.

She followed me on my daily rounds to add to her blackmail arsenal—ammunition to get me to give her something when she wanted it or to do something for her when she wanted me to, or however she wanted to use her secret weapon.

"If you don't give me so-and-so, or let me do so-and-so, I'll tell Mama you play for halves."

I knew why it was called playing for keeps, because you kept what you got. But I never understood why it was called playing for halves, because you never got half of anything. You got all the marbles you won.

I got tired of Ruth following me for her purposes. So one day I told her, "Ruth, if you follow me today, you'll be sorry."

"Nyah, nyah, nyah," she countered, sticking out her tongue.

"All right. Don't say I didn't warn you."

"Nyah, nyah, nyah."

I walked the block to "Miss Thelma" Rutland's store and turned left to go to Mrs. Mainor's, another block away. As soon as I turned the corner, I put the edge of Mama's saucer between my forefinger and thumb and whacked Ruth across the head with it. The saucer shattered to pieces.

Ruth started crying. It must have hurt her head as well as her pride.

"Mama's gonna whip you for this!" she yelled as she started back home.

Whipping was the least of my worries right then. What was I going to do about Mama's best saucer? And Mrs. Mainor's butter? I couldn't do anything about the saucer, but I could about the butter. I had a plan.

"Mrs. Mainor, could you lend me a saucer for the butter? I accidentally dropped Mama's and broke it. I'll bring yours back soon as I get home," I said in my best Sunday School voice.

I got back home with the butter all right. I also got my whipping as Ruth predicted. But it was worth it. She never followed me again. The bad thing, though, I didn't get to play marbles that day.

I think it's a pity more kids don't get whippings these days—at home, and in school. Whippings never harmed my psyche. I got no physical or emotional scars from them. They made me a better boy, and later a better man. I just wish I had gotten more of them. "Spare the rod and spoil the child" is just as true today as it was then.

Ruth and I are the only ones of the seven family members left. We are closer than ever now, even though we live more than 200 miles apart, and see each other rarely. I love her dearly. We still tease each other. I thank the Lord we still can.

Jimmy (James Clarence), born in 1908, was the oldest child. While still a boy he fell into the gravel pit across the street from our East Broad Street home and lost the sight in one eye. It didn't seem to bother him, though, the rest of his long life.

After a short time as a traveling salesman, he became part owner with Perry Horne of a Gulf service station, then part owner with Emmett Jones of another, and finally founder and co-owner with Fain Dykes of the Motor Parts Company.

Jimmy was a 32nd Degree Scottish Rite Mason and Shriner, and an Elder, Sunday School superintendent and choir member of the First Presbyterian Church. He died in 1991 at age 83 after being bed-bound in his West Broad Street home several years with complications from a stroke. His first wife Emmie had also died after a stroke.

Mildred Elizabeth, next oldest, born in 1911, was known for her sweet disposition and winning smile. She was a beauty queen: Miss Eufaula, Miss Alabama, and first runner-up for Miss Dixie. She was a telephone switchboard operator for Southern Bell, then was employed by Schaub's Book Store and Price Drugs.

After her brilliant, handsome husband died in 1948 of a heart attack at age 37, Mildred lived with and took care of Daddy in their Orange Street home, after Mama died, for 17 years until his death. She continued living there 16 more years until she died there of a stroke at age 80 in 1991, the same year Jimmy died.

Evelyn Ruth (Ruth), born in 1920 and still living in Eufaula, worked for years in Whitlock's Jewelry Store under successive owners. As a saleslady, she was much sought after by customers wanting to buy gifts for special occasions.

All her life she has been a faithful, active member of the First Presbyterian Church, and also a Sunday School officer. She has been officially designated by the church as a Lifetime Honorary Member.

William Horace (Horace), the youngest, was born in 1922. He was a Journalism graduate of the University of Alabama and also studied Journalism at Northwestern University, where I got my Master's in Journalism and later taught there. He worked on the Florence Times, and was a combat Infantry officer in Europe in World War II.

After returning home, he became a field director for the American Red Cross, serving in Camp LeJeune, Charleston, Durham, Charlotte, Miami, Jackson and Virginia Beach. He died of a heart attack in 1981 at age 58 while attending a Red Cross convention in Washington, D.C.

All five children were born and reared in Eufaula, graduated from Eufaula High School, and belonged to the First Presbyterian Church.

CHAPTER 9

You Are Going To Sunday School And Church!

My religious upbringing consisted largely in going to Sunday School and church at the First Presbyterian Church, the Christian Endeavor (young people's meeting) Sunday night, and prayer meeting Wednesday night. Mama saw to it that all her chill'un went, religiously—no ifs, ands or buts. No arguments.

The Alabama State Archives in Montgomery records in "Presbyterian Church Histories of the Synod of Alabama, East Alabama Presbytery" that the First Presbyterian Church was organized in 1836 with 16 members.

The first church bell rung in Eufaula was the Presbyterian Church bell. The Rev. James Stratton was the church's first regular minister, coming about the beginning of the year in 1838.

That year, there was a protracted (extended, prolonged) meeting in which the Methodist, Baptist and Presbyterian churches took part, probably the first protracted meeting ever held in Eufaula. It took place in what was then the Jewish Synagogue, which no longer exists.

"There was a remarkable outpouring of the Spirit…. One of the preachers gave a temperance sermon in which he denounced the use of brandy peaches…and the sermon had such an effect that almost the entire population emptied their brandy peaches in the streets and they were eagerly devoured by the hogs. The result was that there were the drunkest set of hogs in Eufaula that day that ever perhaps were seen anywhere."

The present Gothic-style brick building at Randolph Avenue and Church Street was built in 1869 at a cost of $2,200 and dedicated in 1871. Records show that in 1871 prominent Eufaulians L. Y. Dean and C. S. McDowell were ordained Deacons and during 1882-1885 were ordained Elders.

An old wrought-iron fence encloses it. It has a high ceiling with large wooden beams forming crosses, and beautiful old stained-glass windows. Old teardrop-shaped light bulbs shine from the original chandeliers onto the original pews. The church's first Bible is still there.

I love that old church. It was the bed-rock of my boyhood. To a large extent it helped mold my character. Many pastors and members I respected and loved walked down its aisles. There we had our family baptisms, weddings and funerals. It's still my church, and always will be.

Some of its 29 pastors I knew and heard preach were J. D. McPhail; J. Leighton Scott, who was also our Scoutmaster; J. E. Hobson, who scared me and Ruth sometimes with his Hell-fire-and-damnation sermons; C. Walker Sessions, who married Ruth and my Abbeville friend John Fern White one hot July day in 1939 in the manse; John Kirstein, and N. G. Barron.

His son, William G. Barron (Billy when a boy in Eufaula), is now a long-time pastor of the Sequoyah Hills Presbyterian Church in Knoxville, where I was an Elder and Kay and I were members for eight years before Bill came. His mother, "Miss Ruby" Barron, still lives in Eufaula and is a much-beloved member of the First Presbyterian Church.

Fern White later became a Sunday School superintendent in the church, an Elder, and was Clerk of Session, as was my late beloved niece, Betty Cade (Mrs. Van) Smith.

Two of my favorite Sunday School teachers were F. W. Clapp, a transplanted Minnesotan, and L.Y. (Yank) Dean III, local bank president and long-time Sunday School superintendent. His wife, Mary Willie Schaeffer ("T") Dean, was a pianist and organist.

Margaret Jean Brown was an earlier pianist. The Bray sisters, Ethel and Katie, started the church choir and sang in it many years. So did Jimmy, Mildred and Horace at various times.

Perfect Sunday School attendance was rewarded at the end of each church year. You started your attendance record when you were 6 and in the first grade at school, and ended the marathon 12 years later when you graduated from high school.

The first year you got a little round blue and white badge with a red cross in the middle, the second year an imitation-gold wreath to circle the badge, and each year thereafter a colored bar with the year on it to attach to your badge and wreath.

I had perfect attendance all 12 years, and thus a complete ladder of bars, thanks mainly to Mama's persistence. Of course if you were sick on a Sunday it was an excused absence, just like in school. If you were out of town, you had to go to Sunday School wherever you were.

I still have that badge and wreath with 10 bars hanging down. A bit tarnished and a mite rusty. But I cherish them as much as I do my Army medals.

I've never stopped loving those old hymns we sang before Sunday School and during church:

"In the Sweet Bye and Bye," "The Old Rugged Cross," "What a Friend We Have in Jesus," "Blessed Assurance," "Beulah Land," "When They Ring the Golden Bells," "When the Roll Is Called Up Yonder," "Shall We Gather at the River," "Leaning on the Everlasting Arms," "Beautiful Isle of Somewhere," "Precious Memories," "Just a Closer Walk With Thee," "Softly and Tenderly," "Sweet Hour of Prayer," "Bringing in the Sheaves," "Brighten the Corner," "Amazing Grace," "Whispering Hope," "Rock of Ages," "Church in the Wildwood," "I Love to Tell the Story," "Jesus Loves Me," "Ivory Palaces"....

I wish we would sing them now in my Hilton Head Island First Presbyterian Church.

You couldn't join our Eufaula church until you were 12. You were supposed to come every Sunday before then, but you couldn't become a full-fledged member until you reached that magic age and stood before the congregation one Sunday and were examined on the Shorter Catechism by church Elders. They looked stern and formidable and all business, but actually if you could answer the main question you were "in".

That question was, "What is the chief end of Man?" The answer, and I've never forgotten it, is: "The chief end of Man is to glorify God and to enjoy Him forever." That was what the Catechism was all about anyway, and maybe the whole Bible.

After the examination was over, one of the Elders handed me a little Bible with my name written in it, and they all smiled and shook hands with me and welcomed me into the church. That was one of the happiest days of my life. I still have the Bible.

Actually, the mean-looking old Elders weren't so bad after all. I became one myself many years later, and a Deacon. They did perform an important function in the Eufaula church. If you dozed off, or talked or whispered to somebody, or fidgeted too noticeably, one of the Elders would tap you on the shoulder with a long rod to remind you where you were.

There were few Catholics in Eufaula when I was growing up. We had our tales and superstitions about the Catholics, just as I'm sure they had about us Protestants. Even with only a few members, there was, and still is, a Catholic

Church (Holy Redeemer) on the lower part of College Hill on far West Broad Street, then next door to the Pomeroys.

The First Baptist Church had by far the most members, followed by the Methodists, the Presbyterians, the Episcopalians and the Catholics. Most members of the Episcopal Church were old-line, wealthy, aristocratic Eufaulians.

There were even fewer Republicans than Catholics in Eufaula back then, two that I knew of: Mr. and Mrs. H.E. Maugan, Harry and Lillian. Mr. Maugan was the only studio photographer in town, with an upstairs office on downtown Broad Street.

I'm sure many Eufaulians and their descendants still have family pictures with the name H. E. Maugan's Studio on the bottom. Some of mine do.

The rumor was the Maugans moved to Eufaula so they could be postmaster or postmistress when a Republican was President. Sure enough, they alternated the job during Republican presidencies.

In our Eufaula homes as long as I can remember was a maroon, velvet-covered hanging with these gold-colored words etched on it:

> Do nothing
> You would not like to be doing
> When Jesus comes.
>
> Say nothing
> You would not like to be saying
> When Jesus comes.
>
> Go to no place
> Where you would not like to be found
> When Jesus comes.

Not a bad guide for living.

CHAPTER 10

Christmas Was A Happy Time

Charles Dickens wrote in "A Christmas Carol: "I have always thought of Christmas time…as a good time, a kind, forgiving, charitable pleasant time."

Christmas time was just such a happy time for the Cade family, thanks mainly to Mama.

Daddy gave her grocery money each week and she squirreled away some of it in an empty Maxwell House Coffee can in the kitchen to save for Christmas shopping. When the time came to shop, there usually wasn't a whole lot in the can, but without Mama's cleverness, there would have been nothing.

I believed in Santa Claus as long as I could, and pretended to believe for a while after I no longer believed. It was a lot more fun believing. It's a pity children these days learn the truth far too soon. Some are told right from the beginning there is no Santa Claus, when everybody knows there really is.

Mama used stretchy stockings with runs in them to hang up over the fireplace. We usually got an apple, an orange or tangerine, sometimes a banana, Brazil nuts (they were called the now politically incorrect name of nigger toes back then), English walnuts, pecans (better than the ones from the tree in our back yard), bulk raisins still on their stems, and peppermint stick candy. Maybe even a package of baby firecrackers or sparklers, or a handkerchief, or a small puzzle, car or toy.

We got very little for Christmas, but what we got we were happy with. Each of us children usually got at least one new toy or game and some clothes we needed. If we were lucky enough to get a tricycle or bicycle or wagon, it was second-hand and re-painted.

And joy of joys if I got a tan cowboy suit with a cowboy hat and rope and a red-figured bandanna, or a tan, fringed Indian suit with a feathered head-dress and a rubber tomahawk, or a cap pistol with decorated holster and round-roll or single-sheet ammunition caps (depending on the type of pistol), or an only-in-your-dreams Daisy air rifle with BB shots. Ruth might want a doll or a doll-house, a miniature stove with oven, a miniature tea set, or play furniture.

If Mama's coffee can was fuller than usual a particular Christmas, we may have gotten one or more of those extras. If not, back to the basics.

Of course there were gifts from each other, something we hoped the receiver wanted or needed. We watched each other's faces as the presents were opened to see if they liked what they got. We had spent some of the hard-earned money we made working before Christmas to buy them, so they darned well better like what they got. Or at least pretend to.

Mama and Daddy got more expensive presents. Daddy usually got gifts like ties, initialed handkerchiefs, socks, warm cloth gloves, or Mennen's after-shave lotion, older brother Jimmy about the same. Mama got things like initialed hand-kerchiefs, stockings, perfume, scarves, imitation-leather gloves, older sister Mildred about the same—but sometimes also "jewelry" from McCrory's 5 & 10 Cent Store where she worked.

I always got Mama a 25c box of chocolate-covered cherries. I sometimes gave her the same on Mother's Day. I never knew her to offer anybody a piece.

And good old Uncle Loyd. He was a bachelor most of his life, so maybe he had a little more money than his two brothers. Anyway, each Christmas morning when we went down Orange Street to Mother's (my grandmother's) to exchange presents, Uncle Loyd gave each of his nieces and nephews two brand-new dollar bills.

That was a lot of money back then. A week's wages for working in a grocery store or delivering groceries, six days a week. I got only $1.25 a week for delivering the Eufaula Daily Citizen, but I also got free passes to the Lee Theater, because the manager traded passes for ads.

On Christmas morning we had a late big, special, once-a-year breakfast—after we took down our stockings and opened our presents.

Our Christmas dinner, later than usual, was the traditional one, including turkey with corn bread dressing and giblet gravy, jellied cranberry sauce, baked ham with pineapple on top, creamy buttery whipped potatoes with regular gravy, creamy buttery sweet potatoes with toasted marshmallows, ambrosia, home-made Fleischmann's yeast rolls with butter and preserves, home-made vanilla ice cream with chocolate sauce, and a choice of cake from the dozen or so Mama had baked.

Just a light lunch. Supper? Usually turkey sandwiches with hot cocoa, and anything else you wanted from the leftovers—which were left over for several days.

We didn't buy a Christmas tree like people spend a small fortune for now. We went into the woods, hoping it was no one's property or we weren't caught but not really caring, chopped down the best little cedar tree we could find, and carried it home.

It didn't matter if it was scrawny and you could see through it. It was OUR Christmas tree. If we were lucky, we might run across a little fir tree, which was prettier and less scrawny. In either case, the only cost was time and labor.

The tree was decorated about a week before Christmas with large rope-like gray tinsel, small thin silvery icicles, various ornaments collected over the years, and varied-colored lights, all of which covered the flaws in the tree. The bulbs were always burning out, so we kept replacing them with spares kept near the tree. Afterwards the Christmas decorations were stored and saved for the next Christmas.

We hated to take the tree down after Christmas, but it was bad luck to leave it up till New Year's Day, so it came down and was taken to the backyard on December 31—as late in the afternoon as possible. It stayed green awhile, but when it turned brown we set fire to it and enjoyed the warmth and the crackling as it burned. It was a sort of ceremonial burning honoring the good times we had around it.

A nostalgic funeral of sorts.

CHAPTER 11

Growing Up In A Small Southern Town

I loved, and still love, Eufaula.

It is a town of grand old historic ante-bellum and Victorian homes built by 19th-century plantation owners and merchants when "cotton was king" in Eufaula and the rest of the South. Some of those homes still house family heirlooms, symbols of a by-gone era.

It is also a town of old-line churches, fine schools and caring teachers, beautiful trees and flowers, wide streets which weren't paved when I was a boy, nice genteel people—some rich, some poor, some in-between.

Just because you lived in Eufaula didn't mean you were a Eufaulian. You must have been born in Eufaula and your family must have lived in Eufaula for several generations for you to be a true Eufaulian. I consider it an honor and a privilege to be a true Eufaulian.

This story tells how I feel about my home town:

A man decided to write a book about churches in the United States. He started in San Francisco. Going to a large church in that city, he spotted a golden telephone on the vestibule wall and was intrigued by a sign that read, "$10,000 a minute."

Finding the pastor, he asked about the phone and the sign. The pastor said the phone was, in fact, a direct line to Heaven, and if the man paid the price he could talk directly to God.

As he continued to visit churches, going eastward around the country, he found more phones with the same sign, and got the same answer from each pastor.

Finally, he arrived in Eufaula, Alabama. Upon entering the First Presbyterian Church, he saw the usual golden telephone. But this time the sign read "Calls: 25 Cents." Fascinated, he talked with the pastor.

"Reverend, I have been in cities all across the country and in each church I visited I have found a golden telephone and have been told it is a direct line to Heaven and that I could talk to God. But in the other churches the cost was $10,000 a minute. Your sign reads 25 cents a call. Why?"

The pastor replied, "Son, you're in Eufaula now. It's a local call."

The Chattahoochee River, which formed Lake Eufaula after a dam near Fort Gaines, Georgia was completed in 1963, marked Eufaula's eastern boundary and was a state limit as well.

An old, weather-beaten, covered wooden bridge carried walkers, wagons and early-vintage automobiles bound for the flatlands of Georgia and up the hill to the itsy-bitsy town of Georgetown, where it was rumored there were bootleggers. I could name names, but I won't. Some of the families may still be living there.

It was a daring and spooky thing to do to walk across the long, dark, creaky, latticed bridge, musty with age, and look down through wide cracks at the muddy, swirling, swift-flowing, river that rolled south till it joined the Flint River at Chattahoochee, Florida to form the Apalachicola River, which then flowed down to Apalachicola on into the Gulf of Mexico.

The town of Apalachicola had, and still has, probably the best oysters in the world. My wife and I have driven there many miles out of the way just to feast on them—raw, fried and in oyster stew. Eufaula residents have feasted on them since the town was settled, getting them then by steamboats and now by trucks.

The Chattahoochee begins at Chattanooga Gap, 200 yards south of the Appalachian Trail. It is 436 miles long, 262 of them navigable from Columbus, Georgia to Apalachicola.

The most likely origin of its name was in 1799 when Benjamin Hawkins, an Indian agent, wrote in his log that "the name of the river derived from 'chatto', a stone, and "hoche', marked or flowered, there being rocks of this description in the river." In brief, "painted rocks." The site of those rocks, he wrote, was near an Indian village in Georgia named "Chattahoochee," probably near the present town of Franklin in Heard County.

The bridge, 540 feet long, had been built in the early 1830s for $22,000—a lot of money then—when Eufaula was named Irwinton. The builders were John Godwin of Chesterfield, South Carolina and his slave, Horace King, part black, part Indian.

King was born in South Carolina in 1807, the same year Robert E. Lee was born. He was freed in 1846 by an act of the Alabama legislature after Godwin sold him to a Tuscaloosa, Alabama businessman named Jemison, who had a descendant and distant kinsman I knew there named Cade Jemison. King continued to build bridges with Godwin, his good friend and former owner, until Godwin's death.

After that, King, who had developed a reputation as a master bridge-builder, continued his construction work, including the erection of numerous bridges for the Confederacy during the Civil War. After the war, he founded King Brothers Bridge Company.

He served two terms in the post-war Alabama General Assembly and died in 1885 at age 77 in LaGrange, Georgia, where the former slave is buried near the Confederate cemetery.

Sadly, to me at the time, the old wooden bridge was demolished and replaced in 1926 by a concrete one, the Charles S. McDowell Bridge, named for Eufaula's lieutenant-governor, who nine years later encouraged me to enroll at the University of Alabama, where he had graduated from Law School.

A ferry took people, cars and wagons across the river while the new bridge was being built. That bridge, too, was torn down and replaced in 1962 by the wider present-day Richard B. Russell Bridge, named for Georgia's distinguished bachelor United States Senator, whom I had known earlier when I was an Atlanta Journal reporter.

I still remember vividly as a boy walking down the hill from my East Broad Street home to the river to watch paddle-wheeler boats come in loaded with bales of cotton which were unloaded and left on the wharves to be put in warehouses and later shipped down the river to Apalachicola and from there to places like New York City and Liverpool, England.

I can still see the riverboat captains resplendent in their dark-blue uniforms with hard-visor caps, proud pilots of steamboats with such names as the City of Eufaula, the Dixie Belle, the Jubilee, the M. W. Kelly, the W. C. Bradley, the River Queen and the Robert E. Lee. I can still smell the unmistakable odors at the wharves, especially those of damp cotton.

Between 1828 and 1939, more than 200 stern-and side-wheel river boats navigated the Chattahoochee from Columbus to Eufaula to Apalachicola.

Sometimes during the summer right after supper, late in the afternoon when the air was cooling off, some of my friends and I would walk down to the big sandbar jutting into the river under the bridge.

We would carry blankets to sleep on, fishing poles equipped with hooks, lines and sinkers, some dirt-covered wigglers in a tin can, Boy Scout pocket knives to clean the fish we hoped to catch, a small frying pan, some grease in a little jar, and some matches.

If we were lucky, we would fry the fish, mostly catfish, over a fire built with dead tree branches and any other wood we found on the sandbar. Then we would sit around the fire and talk about girls and all that, tell ghost stories, and gab about anything else on our minds.

When we started yawning, we put out the fire, Boy Scout style, lay down on our blankets, maybe kept on talking a bit, then fell asleep, listening to the sounds of the rushing river, far-away train whistles, and other assorted night sounds. In the morning we would wake up after the sun rose, and reluctantly wend our ways home.

I would look up at the steep clay banks, caused by eons of erosion, descending from the Bluff, and think about the Indians who had seen the same sights many years ago.

I have actually seen people eat clay from those banks. We called them dirt-eaters or clay-eaters, attributing their gastronomic proclivity to a vitamin deficiency. Some clay-eaters claimed it settled their stomachs. Some wrapped clay mud around their ankles for poultices, supposedly to ease the pain of sprains.

Clay-eating probably came with the slaves from Africa, where it was a common practice. It used to be widespread in the South for both races, especially among the poor. Long ago clay was eaten to treat various illnesses. Kaolin, a substance akin to clay, is the main ingredient in a well-known, non-prescription medicine.

I wouldn't take anything for growing up in a low-income family in a small town. We never considered ourselves poor. We always had enough clothes, plenty to eat, lots of love for each other, and lots of friends to play with.

I might go with friends to the picture show on Saturday afternoon for a dime (15c after you were 12) to see a serial which always ended with the hero or heroine, in a seemingly inescapable situation, about to die a horrible death—like being gagged and bound with ropes on a railroad track with a train bearing down on the helpless victim just as the movie ended—though I knew he or she would be rescued somehow by somebody just in the nick of time next Saturday. But I wondered for a week how it would happen. That was just the beginning of my dime's worth.

I also got to see a Fox Movietone News, a short comedy (Ben Turpin, Buster Keaton, Harold Lloyd, the Keystone Cops, Our Gang, Laurel and Hardy, etc.) or a Lowell Thomas Travelogue, and then the piece de cinema Western feature starring Tom Mix, Hoot Gibson, Ken Maynard, Tim McCoy, Buck Jones, Jack Hoxie, Randolph Scott, Bob Steele, et al.

Talkies came much later, when the old silent heroes faded away to be replaced by talkers who kissed girls and didn't ride off into the sunset.

Cowboys were our heroes, our role models, back then. I mean the ones in the white hats on the white horses, not the ones in the black hats on the black horses.

Why did we look up to them?

Because they were never looking for trouble, but when it came, they faced it bravely.

They were always on the side of right. They defended good people against bad people.

They had high morals. They had good manners. They were honest.

They spoke their minds and they spoke the truth, regardless of what other people thought.

They were respected. When they walked into a saloon, never to drink the hard stuff, the place became quiet, and the bad guys kept their distance.

If they got in a gunfight, they never killed anyone. They always shot the villain in the arm, or in the foot, or on the leg, or on the trigger hand, never in a vital spot. In a fist-fight, they could beat up anybody.

They always won. They always got their man. But in victory they didn't stay around to take the credit. They rode off into the sunset. Alone.

Would that we had such heroes and role models today!

The first talking picture I saw, when I was about 12, was "Tenderloin," starring Conrad Nagel, a story about San Francisco's notorious crime district. Actually it was only part-talkie. Most of it was silent. But it was billed as "talking."

During the movie, all of a sudden the sound would come on. I never knew when, but I was anticipating when it would be next. When it did, the audience ooohed and aaahed. So I wasn't prepared when Conrad Nagel was in a bar with a drink in his hand and he shook the glass and—the ice tinkled! There was a collective gasp from the audience.

That was my first sound at a movie. After that scene, when the star actually talked, I waited eagerly for the next sound bite.

The sound was by Vitaphone. It wasn't part of the film, but was on a record that was supposed to synchronize with the film. Unfortunately, more times than not, the sound was either ahead of or behind the moving lips. The first full-length talking picture I remember seeing and hearing was Al Jolson in "The Jazz Singer."

When I wasn't playing, I could always go to the Carnegie Library and while away many happy hours, reading Howard Garis' Tom Swift books and Edgar Rice Burroughs' science fiction and Tarzan books, leaving the bounds of Eufaula to travel to a never-never world that was as real to me as the real world.

For some reason the book titles "Tom Swift and the Electric Runabout," "Thuvia, Maid of Mars," "Tarzan of the Apes" and "The Son of Tarzan" stick out in my memories. Wonder if those books are still in the library. Maybe on my next visit....

It was only a short walk from our Orange Street home up Bloom's alley across Randolph Street to St. James Place, where the library's side entrance is located. I had to walk up steps to get in. They seemed steeper then than now, and I recall sitting on them many a Saturday morning waiting for the library to open. Miss Jenny McRae, the librarian, was nice and helpful to a small boy looking for a good book to read.

Early on, sister Mildred had started reading children's picture books to me, including "Grimm's Fairy Tales," "Tales of Hans Christian Anderson" and Joel Chandler Harris' "Uncle Remus." Soon I was reading back to her.

Mildred also taught me the alphabet, how to write, how to spell simple words, and a bit of addition, subtraction and multiplication. In other words, she was my unpaid pre-school and kindergarten teacher As a result, by the time I was 6 I already knew a little about how to read, write, spell and do arithmetic, so after a week or two in the first grade I was sent to the second grade.

I'm sure Mildred and those many hours I spent at the library instilled in me an early love for reading and learning that had a profound influence on my life and my careers. I and many other Eufaulians are deeply indebted to the philanthropist Andrew Carnegie whose gift of $10,000 enabled the library to open its doors in May 1904, nearly 100 years ago.

To me the library looks pretty much the same today as it did when I first went there about 80 years ago, except it's bigger and has more books, of course. Each time I come to Eufaula I manage to find time to go back there. It is holy ground to me.

I almost forgot. When I was in high school I was in a play in the library's auditorium upstairs. I played the role of Obadiah, and Catherine Smith was my pretty sweetheart. One of the songs we sang in the play was a duet, sung as she was sitting in a swing in a frilly white dress. I still remember the words she sang: "Swing me just a little bit higher, Obadiah, do." Who could blame me for having a crush on her?

There was plenty to do when I was growing up. I never got bored, for the day started soon and ended all too soon when I was enjoying life and relishing every minute of it.

In 1920, when I was 3 years old, the U. S. Census population of Eufaula was 4,939. In 1930, when I became a teenager and was in my last year of Junior High, it was 7,418. By 2000, the town had grown to 13,908, and now is edging toward the 15,000 mark.

Go back with me in my mental time machine to Eufaula in the 1920s and 1930s, and re-live with me some kaleidoscopic memories of my boyhood days:

Playing hide-and-go-seek in the dusk. Catching lightning bugs, putting them in jars and watching them light up the jars (good bait for bream, too). Tying strings around the legs of July flies to hear their raucous noise when you whirled them around your head. Sitting on the porch on cool evenings.

Hot home-made yeast rolls and churned butter. Baloney sandwiches. Dill pickles and salt mullet in barrels. Chocolate sodas and malted milk shakes. Cherry Cokes. Vanilla Cokes. Lime Cokes. Plain Cokes. Moon Pies and Eskimo Pies.

Big Baby Ruths for a nickel, little ones for a penny. Blackjack, Clove and Teaberry chewing gum. Wax miniature Coke-shaped bottles with colored sugar water inside. Soft-drink machines that dispensed glass bottles for a nickel. Candy cigarettes. Licorice and stick candy. Jaw breakers. Butterscotch.

Merry-go-rounds and Ferris wheels. School half-holidays for circuses and fairs. Circus parades through town, with elephant droppings galore. Minstrel shows like "Silas Green from New Orleans."

Jacks, horseshoes, buckety-buck, mumblety-peg. Sling-shots. Cork pop-guns. Pea-shooters. Tinker Toys. Erector Sets.

Digging for worms, then wading up and down Chewalla Creek looking for likely fishing holes. When I caught a small bream, I cleaned it with my Boy Scout knife, impaled it on a stick, and cooked it over a little fire.

Lying on my back in the grass with a friend and imagining what the big fluffy clouds looked like: "That one (pointing) looks like a cat." "That one looks like a cow."

Swimming in "Miss Thelma" Rutland's Crystal Pool on Orange Street, or in Irby's Pool north of town, or in ponds, creeks, the river. Anywhere that was wet. The exhilarating feel of that first plunge into the clear, cool water on pool-opening day, knowing I had a season ticket's worth of swimming in the hot summer days ahead of me. Swimming without bathing suits in Chewalla Creek at church picnics, girls and boys in separate swimming holes, chaperones guarding the girls to keep the boys from peeking, nobody guarding the boys because girls didn't peek.

All-day singing with dinner on the ground at country churches. We bad boys would sing: "In the sweet, gimme some meat, bye and pie, gimme some pie, We shall meet on that beautiful shore, gimme some more...."

Cane grindings in the Fall and hog killing at first frost.

Riding in a Model-T Ford on country dirt roads at the breakneck speed of 35 miles an hour.

Selling groceries in Mr. Jim Faulk's store next to the courthouse, and watching the lunch-time crowd eating vienna sausages, potted meat, pickled pig's feet sold from an open barrel, sardines, cheese and crackers. Washed down with a Nehi Orange or Nehi Grape.

Bread and crackers were free. One regular customer was always asking for more bread, so not knowing his name we called him "Mo' Bread." We also had customers named Alabama, Florida and Georgia.

The smell of freshly parched peanuts from the roasting machine in front of Mr. Jim's, attracting an early-morning crowd, including Mr. R. M. McEachern from the courthouse who always picked up a big handful to sample. Mr. Mac Braswell, who specialized in meat, was a competitor a few doors down and lived with his family in the back of his store.

Delivering groceries for Mr. Wilson at his store on East Broad Street near "Miss Thelma" Rutland's store, either on bicycle or on foot, depending on the distance. Some people phoned in their orders, the storekeeper filled them, and I delivered them.

Eating Isaac Warren's mouth-watering hamburgers on Saturday nights at his small stand on Randolph Street during supper break from working at the A & P Food Store around the corner on Broad Street.

Isaac charged 15c for his hamburgers, a nickel more than others charged, but it was well worth it. The taste couldn't be duplicated. Neither could the savory odor emanating from the stand as you neared it. I haven't had as good a hamburger since, and probably never will.

Eating a pint of cold, raw Apalachicola oysters at the A & P after I got back from Isaac Warren's.

Telephone party lines with several families on the line and the inconveniences that sometimes caused, much less eavesdropping. Eufaula's Southern Bell telephone office was upstairs in a Broad Street building, where several switchboard operators, including Mildred, plugged reddish phone lines into switchboard holes to connect callers.

Washtubs with wringers. Clothes draped across a long wire connected to two posts in the backyard to dry them. Singer treadle sewing machines. Home milk delivery in returnable glass bottles with cardboard stoppers.

Going to proms and trying to fill as many spaces as possible on your prom card with that special girl who wore such good-smelling perfume. Exchanging Valentines—romantic and comic—and signing them guess who.

When pre-teen boys pretended not to like girls, and pre-teen girls pretended not to like boys.

Boys sang this little song: "Reuben, Reuben I've been thinking, What a great world this would be, If the girls were all transported, Far beyond the Northern Sea." Girls sang the same song, changing Reuben to Rachel and girls to boys.

When around the corner seemed far away, and going downtown like going somewhere. A trip to exotic places like Columbus, Dothan and Montgomery was for later in life, and to Birmingham for much later. Anybody who lived north of Birmingham was a suspect Yankee.

Trapping little green snakes in cigar boxes held up by a stick and yanked with a string when the prey went inside to eat the lettuce or other greenery that made the snakes green, then putting the snake inside your buttoned-up and tucked-in shirt and feeling it slithering around trying to get out.

Climbing trees. Sticky fingers from Lord knows what. A million mosquito bites over the years.

Trying to read and study by flickering kerosene lamps because we had no electricity, and getting up early to study when I could see better. Bedtime came early, before our first electric light bulbs hung bare from the ceiling.

Trying to stay awake long enough to wash my always dirty feet before going to bed, only because Mama made me do it. In Eufaula, boys went barefoot from about March to November, the joyful taking-off-your-shoes and reluctantly putting-them-back-on times depending on the temperature. Most girls wore shoes all the time, except for a few tomboys and unconventional exceptions.

Bathing in a big washtub in front of the fire on cold Saturday nights and on any other nights Mama said I needed to, which was too often—freezing on one side, burning up on the other.

Getting water for all uses—drinking, bathing, cooking—from a backyard well in all kinds of weather. Running in the winter down a narrow path to and from the outdoor three-seater, and not dallying inside or outside.

Playing cops and robbers. Cowboys and Indians. Running till I was out of breath. Running through hose water. Laughing so hard my stomach hurt. Being tired from playing, and from not playing.

Jumping down the steps. Jumping up the steps. Jumping on the bouncy bed. Just jumping for joy. Pillow fights. Being tickled till it hurt, and tickling my tormentor in turn.

Running home as fast as I could at night down the middle of Orange Street past dark and spooky Dowling's Funeral Home after watching a scary picture show.

Churning sweet milk in a large ceramic jug, light tan with a dark brown-colored ring near the top, to make buttermilk and butter. Turning till my arm muscles got sore the hard-to-turn handle of a metal rotating ice-cream freezer, packed tightly in chunks of ice and rock salt, to produce a velvety creamy miracle with a vanilla flavor.

Running after the horse-drawn ice wagon in the summer to cool off by eating the ice shavings on the back of the wagon, and rubbing them on my hot face and body.

Ice-men delivered ice by weight for wooden home ice-boxes, estimating how much to saw from larger blocks to fill the customer's order. Hence the ice shavings. Or getting the ice-plant owner to let me go inside the large freezer room where the ice was stored so I could really cool off.

Trying to keep cool at home on hot summer days and nights by keeping all the windows open and hoping for a stray breeze.

When we got electricity we used small rotating fans to catch cool air intermittently. Air-conditioning came much later, but for us only a window air-conditioner at the back of the house which somewhat cooled the rest of the house. We never had central air-conditioning in any house we lived in.

Sitting on the curb of unpaved downtown Broad Street and watching my world go by.

The feeling of joy when I found a penny lying in the street, more joy over a nickel, and pure elation over a dime. That was movie money. I could buy a piece of stick candy for a penny or even a small candy bar.

Nowadays most people won't even bother to pick up a penny. Then I'd reach into a muddy gutter for one. A quarter a week was a large allowance. More likely a dime. In my case nothing. No work, no money.

When girls neither dated nor kissed till late high school...if then. Holding hands was heavenly. And if girls smoked or, horrors, drank, they were considered "fast" and fair game.

When men teachers (what few there were) wore neckties and usually coats, and lady teachers had their hair done every day and wore heels and long sleeves. Pupils were kept back a grade if they failed. No social promotions then. Having a weapon in school meant being caught with a sling-shot.

All my teachers were my favorite teachers, except some were more favorite then others: Miss Mattie Walker, Miss Bessie Hayles, Miss Stella Drewry, Miss Ethel Blackmon, Miss Loulie Shelley, Miss Sally Smith, Miss Julia Neighbors, Miss Verdalee Johnson, Miss Ida Foy Pitts Moulthrop, Miss Mignonne Pitts, Miss Annie Ballowe, Coach (and Principal and Chief Paddler) T. J. Campbell, Mrs. Agnes Wilkinson (music, chorus and orchestra teacher).

We called all our teachers Miss, married or not, except Mrs. Wilkinson, who was the superintendent's wife. My Number 1 teacher, of course, was Mama.

When mamas were at home when the school children got there.

When any parent could discipline a child and nobody—not even the child—thought anything about it. Being sent to the principal's office for a whipping or a reprimand was nothing compared with the fate that awaited you at home when you handed over the principal's note. We were in fear of life and limb. "My Mama will kill me when she finds out I did this."

If you have memories of your own from three generations ago, similar to or different from mine, pass them on to people you care about, especially your children and grandchildren.

Don't let those precious memories fade away before it's too late. Like an old photograph. Or dust in the wind.

How could those of us who grew up in the '20s and '30s possibly have survived?

We had no child-proof lids on medicine bottles, or locks on doors or cabinets. When we rode our bicycles we had no helmets.

We tricked-or-treated around town on Halloween night without adults going with us, filling our bags with treats and eating them as we walked along without worrying about what was inside them.

We drank water from creeks or wells or even from the river, and not from a bottle. Our milk was not pasteurized. We ate cakes, cookies, candy, fried fatback for breakfast along with biscuits (made with pure lard) and gravy, and drank sugar-saturated Nehi drinks, Nu-Grapes or Cokes.

But we were never overweight because we were always outside playing instead of watching television or playing games on computers as children do today.

We shared soft drinks, from one bottle, and no one actually died from this.

We had friends. We went outside and found them. We left home in the morning and played all day, as long as we were back when the street lights came on.

We fell out of trees, got multiple cuts and bruises, a few broken bones and sometimes teeth. We had fights and punched each other like the be-jesus, bloodied each other's noses, then shook hands and put our arms around each other and became friends again.

We made up games with sticks and tin cans, games like shinny, and though we were told it would happen, we never put out any eyes.

We petted stray dogs and cats without worrying whether they might have rabies. They weren't given rabies shots back then.

We shot off fireworks without supervision. We walked or rode our bicycles to school or to deliver newspapers or groceries in the flaming heat, in the freezing cold, and in the pouring rain. We left our bicycles lying in the middle of the front yard without worrying about somebody stealing them.

We worked for nothing if it would help us get a job later for pay. I started my newspaper career during high school by asking the Eufaula Tribune managing editor, Mr. W. S. Croker, if he would let me sweep the pressroom floor in exchange for "hanging around" the newspaper. Publisher H. L. Upshaw later hired me as a reporter, and the rest is history for me.

Other Tribune employees I learned from and admired were "Miss Willie" Copeland Couric, my cousin, society editor; "Miss Mae Witt" Smith, circulation manager, and Eudell Monk, pressman.

We were responsible for our actions. We expected, and usually got, consequences. The idea of parents bailing us out if we got in trouble in school or broke a law was unheard of. They actually sided with the school or the law. Imagine that!

Those times so long ago produced some of the best risk-takers ever, because we lived with risks daily. We learned how to take our lumps and bruises and live with them.

And we're still alive. At least some of us still are.

How I wish I could turn back the clock for my children and grandchildren!

Most of my boyhood friends, relatives and townspeople I knew are gone now. The biggest tragedy of my boyhood occurred when a classmate and one of my best friends, Ri (for Rinaldo) Caldwell, was killed in an automobile accident at the early age of 15.

He was driving his Model-T Ford with the top down on the Country Club road, rounded a curve perhaps a bit too sharply, and ran off the road. The car went down the bank, turned over several times and pinned him underneath with a broken neck.

Earlier in the day, Ri had asked me if I wanted to go riding with him, but I had to deliver newspapers that afternoon. When I got home, I heard the news. I remember going to the swing on the front porch and crying till there were no more tears left.

When I saw Ri's body in the casket at the Caldwell home at the foot of College Hill next door to the Pomeroys, I experienced for the first time the finality and utter desolation of death.

No more would I be able to tell Mama, "Me and Ri and Robert (Flewellen)" did so-and-so. Nor hear Ri playing his cornet in the school band and orchestra.

One of my wife Kay's paternal ancestors, Henry Woodman, whose father was a soldier with General George Washington at Valley Forge during the terrible winters of 1777 and 1778, wrote "The History of Valley Forge" in 1850. In it he eloquently described one's youthful years:

"Oh, happy days, now past and gone forever…days of my youth, when perplexing cares and disquietude came not near my dwelling, when earth's engrossing cares and entanglements were strangers, and the ingratitude of man to his fellow-man was unknown."

Henry Wadsworth Longfellow must have been thinking of such a town as Eufaula when he wrote his nostalgic poem, "My Lost Youth". These excerpts reflect my recollections and sentiments about my old home town:

> Often I think of the beautiful town…
> The pleasant streets of that dear old town,
> And my youth comes back to me…
> I can see the shadowy lines of its trees…
> I remember the black wharves and the ships…
> And the beauty and mystery of the ships…
> I can see the breezy dome of groves…
> And the friendships old and the early loves
> Come back with a Sabbath sound, as of doves
> In quiet neighborhoods…
> I remember the gleams and glooms that dart
> Across the school-boy's brain,
> The song and the silence in the heart,
> That are prophecies, and in part
> Are longings wild and vain.…
> There are dreams that cannot die,
> There are things of which I may not speak,
> There are thoughts that make the strong heart weak,
> And bring a pallor into the cheek.…
> Strange to me now are the forms I meet
> When I visit the dear old town,
> But the native air is pure and sweet,
> And the trees that o'ershadow the street,
> As they balance up and down…
> And with joy that is almost pain
> My heart goes back to wander there,
> And among the dreams of the days that were,
> I find my lost youth again.
> And the strange and beautiful song,
> The groves are repeating it still:
> "A boy's will is the wind's will,
> And the thoughts of youth are long, long thoughts."

CHAPTER 12

Dr. McCoo, Aunt Lou And Uncle Matt

I was born in 1917 in the old Hortman home on East Broad Street, a house long since torn down. Many babies were born back then in homes, not in hospitals, and were delivered by mid-wives, not by doctors. Later we moved to an old two-story yellow house at 623 East Broad Street nearer the Bluff, that house also now long gone.

In 1927 when I was 9 we moved uptown to a house Daddy bought from W. Y. Johnston (built about 1870-75) at 226 Orange Street in Eufaula's Historic Seth Lore District, which meant shorter walks to and from school. The town's first four streets were Livingston, Orange, Randolph and Eufaula. The first letters spelled the early developer's name: L-O-R-E.

I was the middle one in a family of five children. There would have been six, but Ellis Martin Cade died in 1914 when he was about 3 months old.

Dr. William Preston Copeland, from whom I got my middle name (Daddy didn't have one, nor did his grandfather for whom he was named)), brought me into the world. He was a first cousin once removed of my paternal grandmother, "Miss Carrie" (Carolyn Elizabeth) Martin Cade, whom we called Mother.

She therefore was a cousin of "Miss Caro" (also Carolyn Elizabeth) Copeland Clayton, Eufaula's beloved matriarch, aptly described in the title of Robert Flewellen's book about her as "Eufaula's Gracious Lady." I cherish the letters I received from her. She always called me "Cousin Dozier." She lived to be 100, and less than a month short of 101.

She and Mother were descendants of John Adam Treutlen, a Salzburger, the first governor of Georgia, who was murdered by some Tories near Orangeburg, South Carolina during the American Revolution. A monument to him stands near Orangeburg.

Dr. Copeland had fought the Yankees when they invaded Tuscaloosa while he was a student at the University of Alabama. He let me ride with him in his horse and buggy while he made his daily rounds to visit sick patients. I used to brag to playmates that Dr. Copeland let me carry his satchel. I idolized that man, and thought about becoming a doctor because of him.

After Dr. Copeland died, there were three excellent doctors and two fine hospitals in our small town. The town was divided into three parts as far as doctors were concerned. If you were white, you were either a Dr. W. S. Britt patient or a Dr. P. P. Salter patient. Britt's Infirmary was on College Hill, Salter's Hospital on the Bluff on Riverside Drive, a short walking distance from our house.

The third doctor was Dr. T. V. McCoo, but because of the color of his skin, his patients were mostly black. However, when Daddy had a skin problem, he always went to Dr. McCoo.

Like other black citizens, when Dr. McCoo went to a picture show he would sit in the balcony. However, when a patient needed him the ushers had a hard time finding him in the dark, so the manager asked him to please sit downstairs. Thereafter he always sat in the first seat in the back row on the left-hand side of the theater so he could be easily located.

The light from the outside lobby shone in on him a bit, and I often wondered if he could see the movie as well as the rest of us could.

Incidentally, Dr. McCoo was the grandfather of Marilyn McCoo, the famous popular singer. So without him we wouldn't have had her beautiful voice.

The town honored his memory by naming a street after him and also a municipal complex, the former T. V. McCoo School. His name also is memorialized by the McCoo branch of the Carnegie Library in the Chattahoochee Courts. His portrait hangs there.

About the time I was born, Mama caught the flu during a worldwide epidemic of the deadly sickness, so she wasn't able to nurse me. Fortunately a family friend, Aunt Lou, also had recently had a baby. When she heard about Mama's situation, she said she had enough milk to feed me and her baby. So my first food came from suckling at the breast of this half-Indian, half-Negro woman.

Naturally we became very close as I grew up. She called me her little papoose. She taught me how to fish, how to catch lightning bugs and doodlebugs.

Doodlebugs live in relative coolness mainly under houses and burrow themselves into loose sand to get cooler, leaving inverted volcano-shaped holes.

To catch them you take the stalk of a weed, spit plentifully on the lower part, stick it in the sand at the bottom of the burrow, twist it, pull it up slowly, and up comes a fat juicy doodlebug—actually the larva of a tumblebug.

Aunt Lou dipped snuff and chewed tobacco. She spit on her baited hook before she cast the line into the water. She said it made the fish bite better. She did catch lots of fish, so who knows?

I still remember Aunt Lou's hand-me-down tales of her Indian ancestors, sometimes called Creeks because they usually lived along creeks to fish in and to get water from and to bathe in. They settled the land that later became Eufaula, or Yufala in their language, which probably meant "high bluff." Eufaula sometimes is referred to as the "Bluff City."

Indians lived in the area from prehistoric times. Over the years, hundreds of villages, ranging from a few to thousands of inhabitants, lined the banks of the Chattahoochee. The Creek brave was tall, lean and muscular, and wore a feathered warlock. When not hunting or fighting, his life was centered in his home village. The mother town of the Creeks in the area was on what is now St. Francis Point.

Looking for fertile cropland, the first white settler, Carson Winslett, moved from Georgia into the Indian village called Eufaula across Chewalla Creek. Others soon followed. Things were peaceful for a while, until incoming whites infringed on Indian lands. A conflict over land led to the bloody Creek Indian war, which ended when the Creeks ceded land to the whites in an 1832 treaty.

Actually it was a treaty of evacuation. Peace came at a price. The Eufaula Creeks literally were driven from their ancestral homes by their more powerful white neighbors, and made the long trek westward to Oklahoma, the last ones leaving in 1837.

They founded Eufaula, Oklahoma, still largely Indian, which has a Lake Eufaula as does their old Eufaula. Kay and I have visited there. Only two towns in the United States have that name.

The Trail of Tears in 1836 led thousands of Creek Indians through Tuskaloosa (now Tuscaloosa), then the capital of Alabama. In a brief but eloquent and poignant speech, Chief Eufaula addressed the Alabama legislature:

"I come here, brothers, to see the great house of Alabama and the men who make laws to say farewell in brotherly kindness before I go to the far west, where my people are now going. In time gone by I have thought that the white man wanted to bring burden and ache of heart among my people in driving them from their homes and yoking them with laws they do not understand. But I have now become satisfied that they are not unfriendly toward us, but that they wish us well. In these lands of Alabama, which have belonged to my forefathers and where their bones lie buried, I see that the Indian fires are going out. Soon they will be cold. New fires are lighting in the west for us, they say, and we will go there. I do not believe our great Father means to harm his red children, but that he wishes us well. We leave behind our good will to the people of Alabama who build the great houses and to the men who make the laws. That is all I have to say."

The Treaty of 1832 led to the creation of Barbour County and the town of Eufaula, which was then known as Irwinton in honor of General William Irwin of nearby Henry County, a War of 1812 hero. He established the first steamboat wharf below the bluff, setting the stage for the town to become a cotton trade center.

But Irwinton lasted only 11 years. The name was changed because a Georgia town had the same name, and the mail got mixed up. It was re-named Eufaula in 1843.

Eufaula grew rapidly and soon became a center of commerce and agriculture, a major hub of shipping and trading. All roads led to Eufaula. Its economy was based on land, cotton and slaves. The building of the covered bridge across the Chattahoochee was a big asset to the town's growth.

I well remember one warm day in June 1923 when I was 5. The town was celebrating Centennial Day, commemorating the founding of Eufaula. No one knows the exact year the town was actually founded, but somehow 1823, four years after Alabama became a state, was settled on as the founding date.

I rode in Mr. John Copeland's open-air Model-T Ford with my sister Mildred, brother Jimmy, and cousins John Vining and Teenie, Edith and Edwin Beverly. I was dressed up in my Indian suit resplendent with feathered headdress. For one day, at least, I WAS Aunt Lou's little Indian boy.

An oft-repeated story of how Eufaula got its name goes like this: An Indian brave and an Indian maiden were standing near the edge of the bluff, and the young girl got too close to the edge. "Watch out!" the young man yelled. "U-fall-uh!"

We also had a Negro friend, Matt (for Matthew) Cade, whom we considered one of the family. As indeed he was, by his heritage. Uncle Matt, as we called him, lived north of Eufaula in Batesville, where Daddy was born.

Daddy and his family had moved from there to Eufaula in 1898 when he was 14, bringing the Cade family Bible with them, which I now have. The first birth recorded in it was Daddy's father, James Smith Cade, in 1855. The last entry was Mama's death 103 years later.

Uncle Matt's family had been slaves in the Cade family, and evidently it was a good relationship because Uncle Matt often talked about how good the Cades had been to his family, both during and after slavery.

He was more than 100 years old in 1948, the last time my wife Kay and I saw him in Eufaula. He was still a spry little fellow with a gray mustache, hat cocked a bit to the right side, and able to get around as well as anybody. He was in Eufaula on his annual pilgrimage to visit the extended Cade family and to get clothes or other necessities from the family.

"Now Mistuh Johnny, he done gimme some shirts, and Mistuh Loyd, he done gimme some pants, now Mistuh Dozier, you needs to gimme a overcoat," he told Daddy on the porch of our Orange Street home. So Daddy and Uncle Matt walked downtown to a clothing store and Daddy bought him an overcoat.

Back home, Uncle Matt told me and Kay: "De Cade fam'ly has al'ays been good tuh me, an' I 'spect dem tuh hep take keh o' me de rest o' mah nachul-bawn days."

Uncle Matt never asked for money. He never asked for much of anything except once a year. But whatever he asked for, Daddy and his brothers gave him. Without question. After all, he was family.

I wish I could have spent more time with Uncle Matt to talk about what it was like in the old days when he was a young slave. But I saw him precious few times. I was the loser for that.

LAST CHAPTER

Goodbye, Mama

With a household of seven, Mama was busy all the time, from sunup to way after supper. No one ever worked harder. She seemed to be able to do ten things at a time.

When she was sick, she never complained but kept on working. When she had to go to bed, I knew she was really sick. Later in life she had bad arthritis in her hands, which she needed most for her endless chores.

I used to see her before breakfast letting hot water run over her hands at the sink so she could move her fingers. She probably had been having chest pains before her fatal heart attack, but hadn't told anybody if she had. She died in Salter's Hospital on the Bluff, not far from where we once lived.

Every time I think about all the things Mama did for her family, and how hard she worked all her life, I think of these words in the Book of Proverbs:

"She rises while it is yet night and provides food for her household.... She opens her mouth with wisdom, and the teaching of kindness is on her tongue. She looks well to the ways of her household, and does not eat the bread of idleness. Her children rise up and call her blessed."

Another Bible verse reminds me of Mama:

"Let not yours be the outward adorning with braiding of hair, decoration of gold, and wearing of fine clothing, but let it be the hidden person of the heart with the imperishable jewel of a gentle and quiet spirit."

I didn't go out much on school nights. I had to stay home and study. Maybe sometimes I went out supposedly to study with a girl I liked, but my mind really wasn't on studying then. Sometimes I could go to an early picture show if I had already studied. But regardless of when I went out, on school nights or weekends or during vacations, I had to be in by 10 o'clock. If I wasn't home by then, I had some explaining to do.

One of my lasting memories of Mama was her always staying up till I got home, even after I was a grown-up and married and came home on visits. In a way it was nice because it meant she loved me and couldn't rest until she knew I was home safe. But in another way I hated for her to have to lose her early sleep because I knew she was tired from working all day. So I tried to get home a little early if I could.

When Mama died when I was 40, people from all over came to the house, church and Fairview Cemetery, where most of our family are buried. It was a short ride to the Orange Street entrance to the cemetery. The family plot is near the entrance.

There was so much food at the house from friends, relatives, neighbors and other townspeople that we had to phone people later to come take some of it before it spoiled. "Miss Caro" Clayton walked all the way from her Cherry Street home to bring some of her home-made yeast rolls, still warm. Before the funeral, a Negro friend and neighbor had come to the house and shooed all the family workers out of the kitchen and took over the food job herself.

Two of my cousins, Teenie and Edith Beverly, sang Mama's favorite hymn, "The Old Rugged Cross," at her funeral in the First Presbyterian Church. (Her favorite secular song was "My Blue Heaven.") They had a hard time getting through it. We all did, but it wouldn't have been Mama's funeral without that hymn.

Mildred usually sang with them. But not that day. The whole service literally was a blur to me because my eyes were full of tears. I felt empty inside. I was empty inside. Time has eased that emptiness some, but not altogether.

Blacks, whites, young, old, Catholics, Protestants, Jews—they all came. Flowers were all over the place. We planted some of the flowering plants later in the front yard and the back yard.

One particular plant produced large, beautiful hydrangeas that graced our front yard for years. The big blossoms changed colors over the years, depending on the nature of the soil, the degree of alkalinity or acidity at the time. We always had this reminder of Mama with us.

I loved Daddy very much, but I always felt closer to Mama. Maybe it was partly because I spent more time with her. After Mildred died, the house on Orange Street (by then Orange Avenue) was sold. The Cade family had lived there 65 years. But it was all over now.

The last time I drove by the old house it was hard for me to look at it. So much love, so many happy memories, so many happy times that no longer live there but now live only in my heart.

I never knew much about Mama's family and relatives. We did visit Enterprise occasionally to see her two brothers and their families, Uncle Horace (Enterprise fire chief for whom my brother Horace was named) and Uncle Neal, and her sister, Aunt Dove. Now and then Aunt Beatrice, who lived way out in Oelrichs, South Dakota, would come see us.

Both of Mama's parents were dead, so I never knew them. I did know her daddy was named James (Jim) Ellis. Daddy's father and my brother also were named James, as is our son James (Jim) Ellis Cade.

Sometimes children listen to or watch what their mamas are saying or doing. Children are more apt to do as their mamas do, not as they say. Mamas are remembered more by their kind deeds than by their kind words.

When you didn't know I was watching you, Mama:

I saw you feed a scraggly, mangy-looking old stray cat, so I learned I should be kind to animals.

I saw tears in your eyes, so I learned it's all right to cry when you want to.

I saw you make my favorite coconut cake, so I learned that the little things could be the best things in life.

I felt you kiss me good night, so I felt loved and secure.

I saw you make a macaroni and cheese casserole to take to a sick neighbor, so I learned I should help take care of other people.

I saw you take care of our house and everyone and everything in it, so I learned I should take care of those I love and what I have.

I learned most of life's lessons that I needed to know from you—mainly how to be like you when I grew up.

Now I would like to be able to look at you, Mama, and say, "Thanks for all the things I saw and heard when you didn't know I was watching and listening."

> I do not know how long I'll live,
> But while I live, please let me give
> Some comfort to someone in need,
> By smile or nod, kind word or deed.
> And let me do what e'er I can
> To ease things for my fellow man,
> I want naught but to do my part
> To lift a tired or weary heart,
> To change folks' frowns to smiles again,
> Then I will not have lived in vain.

And I'll not care how long I live
If I can give…and give…and give.

As you did all your life, Mama, until your heart gave out from so much giving.

EPILOGUE

Life is all about love.

The essence of love is not what we think or do or provide for others, but how much we give of ourselves.

Love leaves a legacy. How you treated other people, not your wealth or accomplishments, is the most enduring impact your life can leave on earth.

As Mother Teresa said, "It's not what you do but how much love you put into it that matters."

Love is the secret of a lasting heritage.

That is your heritage to me, Mama.

A young man walking down a deserted beach just before dawn saw a frail old woman in the distance.

As he approached the woman, he saw her picking up stranded sand dollars and throwing them back in the ocean.

The young man gazed in wonder as the woman again and again threw the small creatures into the water.

"Old woman," he asked, "why do you spend so much time and energy doing what seems a waste of time?"

The woman explained that the sand dollars would die if left in the hot sun.

"But there must be thousands of beaches and millions of sand dollars!" the young man exclaimed. "How can you make a difference?"

The woman looked at the sand dollar in her hand.

"It makes a difference to this one!"

You too made a difference, Mama. In one life and in the lives of many others. That's why I wrote this book in your memory.

UNFOLDING MY LIFE

Students in our 10th Grade English Class were assigned to write their life story in book form, including pictures. Here are the contents of my book with the factual, spelling and style errors just as they were written. Note also my use of stilted language and big words designed to impress my teacher.

*   *   *

"Unfolding My Life"

Dedication

I hereby dedicate this, the story of my life, to my dear mother, who so diligently helped me unfold my past life and helped me with the effective illustrations in this book.

Dozier Cade, Jr.

Preface

The three outstanding purposes of this book are: to help recall the past to my memory in an accurate way, that I may look back on my life in the future, to portray to my friends and relatives the related events of my life.

In this book are illustrations given me by my family and friends, and my hopes and ambitions for the future.

I Growing Up

To me my childhood is most vague part of my life. I remember but a few things, my mother helping me recall the rest.

I was born early in the morning of an Indian Summer day, September 8, 1917, in a two-story yellow house in Eufaula, Alabama, and was christened Dozier Copeland Cade, my first name for my father, my second for the doctor who brought me into the world. He said he would give me his "satchel" when he died. My annual Christmas present from him was a peck of delicious pecans. My first coherible word was "turkey." After that, talking became easy for me. I had my first real picture taken at the age of 8 months at Maugan's studio. It was a difficult task for the photographer, because I was laughing and jumping around. I had a bad habit of putting anything I could pick up into my mouth. This fault was corrected by putting soap on intimate things around me. I received little scolding in my baby days. My brother and sister teased and frightened me so that by the time I was 3 years old I was afraid of the slightest noise. I would crawl under the bed when firecrackers were shot on Christmas day. In the middle of the night I would awaken and ask my mother to turn on the light. While my mother was ill, my old negro mammy, Aunt Lou, would ably take care of me. My favorite toy was a mechanical train. I spent many happy hours seeing how this worked. I was very fond of the neighbors next door, Mr. and Mrs. Copeland, and they of me. I stayed there about half of the daytime, but not at night. When three years old, I was taken to Montgomery by them, who bought me a teddy bear suit, and a life-like teddy-bear. Upon my arrival home I had my picture taken in my suit. About this time I had my black curls removed. At the age of 5 years, I went to my first circus, held in Eufaula at Comer Park. The animals terrified me with their loud bellowing. Of course, there was popcorn and peanuts for all. My last happy event before embarking upon the sea of learning, full of tempests and calms, was a birthday party, given me by my parents on my 6th birthday, about a week before school began. I was the recipient of many lovely gifts, one, a book, whose appellation is "The Little Brown Bear," I still possess. I received books, games, and my first knife and watch.

II My Family and Pets

My family and pets constituted a larger part of my environment because there were few children around me to make acquaintances with.

There were, primarily, 8 people in our immediate family. They were, in order, my father, Dozier, Sr., my mother, Love Ellis, the children, James Clarence (who is now married), named for my paternal grandfather, Mildred Elizabeth, Ellis Martin (who died at the age of 4 months), named for my maternal grandfather, myself, Evelyn Ruth, and last, but not least, William Horace. I was petted by James and Mildred, carried places without asking, and was made much of. All of my grandparents are now dead. We had a family reunion each year until my grandmother's death in 1928, when a massive Christmas tree ornamented with gifts was at the house of the host. It has always been a pleasant memory.

I have had many and varied pets in my short life. My first pet was a hen with her brood of chicks. I have always held a warm place in my life-beating heart for all stray animals, feeding many a hungry cat or dog. A dog can be your best friend or your worst enemy, according to the way they are treated. Kindness is the best policy. I had a devoted canine friend of the bulldog breed who died giving birth to a litter of pups. It was a sad day in my life. I had a large yellow cat named Bill who would follow me around. We had some exciting times with each other. I am especially fond of chickens. I have one pet chicken which was brought from a negro for a dime. This chicken was puny, weighing only 4 ounces. Now it is very healthy, weighing 2½ pounds. After careful training I taught her to jump upon my back to get food out of my hand. Some of my other pets were a guinea, rat, and flying squirrel. My cat devoured the flying squirrel. She must have thought it to be a rat. When I was small I wanted to make a pet out of everything, snakes, toads, frogs, rats, and almost every creeping creature. I soon was taught better.

III School Days

I entered school September, 1923, right after my 6th birthday. My larger sister, Mildred, carried me on my first day. At first I was very hungry and cried to go home, but soon got over my baby ways. My teachers in the first grade were Misses Hollingsworth and Mattie Walker. I had little time to profit by their teaching because, at the end of 2 weeks I was promoted to the 2nd grade. My teacher was Miss Bessie Hayles. It was in this grade that I had my first real sickness. I was in bed with the measles for a month, recuperating by Christmas day. (I had to.) The next year, in Miss Stella Drewry's room, I learned to appreciate the value of music and art, making several clever booklets. I also learned to recite poems. In this grade I was picked on by larger boys. I would want to go home very badly at these times. Miss Ethel Blackmon was my teacher in the 4th grade. We started spelling matches and history in this grade. In the 5th grade, Miss Loulie Shelly was teacher. She had trouble often locating her glasses. No wonder, they were in the back of her hair. Next came a most interesting grade. My teacher in the last grade of grammar school was Miss Sallie Smith. We had lively debates and long speeches, dutifully preparing us for the work ahead. About this time we moved to our present home on Orange Street. We used to thrill over having the highest percentage in attendance and getting a half holiday. Ri Caldwell, Robert Flewellen, and myself had made all "A's" in Grammar school. We were now entering a new and fascinating world.

My debut into the 7th grade was impressive. I received very little hazing, on account of a new ruling about this. This grade was full of studies, with no vacant periods. Mrs. Wilkinson started the school orchestra in this grade. I play the violin. My teachers were Misses Fuller, Smith, and Collins. The 8th grade was very different. I had only 4 subjects to carry. I made my first "B" in this grade. Now for my freshman year. I made my first "B" in English. I won a prize for the best Civics notebook. This grade was different, and was full of ups and downs for me.

The faculty was Mesdames Moulthrop, Pitts, and Ballowe, Miss Neighbors, and Miss Collins. The 10th grade curriculum was hard to get straightened out. We started supervised study. My new teacher, Coach Campbell, is very interesting. I have not been absent or tardy for 3 years up to now. As I recall the days gone by, I envy every child starting in the first grade.

IV Peering Into the Future

I have two predominant ambitions. One is to be a newspaper reporter (especially a sports reporter) for a large newspaper, such as the Chicago Tribune. The other is to be an eminent astronomer. These occupations are very different. I intend to decide first on my career before deciding on the college that I will go to. First I must graduate from high school. I intend to finish with 21 credits. I am going to try for a scholarship. If one is not forthcoming, I hope to work my way through college by the use of my violin, or by odd jobs. I would like first to go to Auburn, then taper off with Harvard. Later, if I have enough money to retire satisfactorily on, I intend to travel, to see America first, then visit historic and interesting places about which I have studied at school. Astronomy has always held a sort of fascination over me. The Unknown has always held sway over me as if by some supernatural power. I would like to study how everything was made, how the objects in the universe are related. My ambition as a journalist was brought about by my intense devotion to the reading of newspapers, especially the sports sections. I would like to be a second Walter Camp. How to decide on a career is a very difficult thing.

*   *   *

Author's Note

I did become a newspaper reporter. I did write sports. I did work on a Chicago newspaper, but it was briefly for the Chicago Daily News, not the Chicago Tribune. I did finish high school with 21 units. I did work my way through college "by odd jobs," but I didn't go to Auburn. Auburn didn't have a Journalism program, the University of Alabama did. I did travel with wife Kay, seeing much of America first and visiting "historic and interesting places" in the States and abroad I had studied about at school. I still love astronomy, and anything about space. Finally, "the Unknown" and supernatural still fascinate me. I have had some profound Extra-Sensory Perception (ESP) experiences that would boggle the mind. Overall, not bad for prognostication.

My First Picture, with Daddy

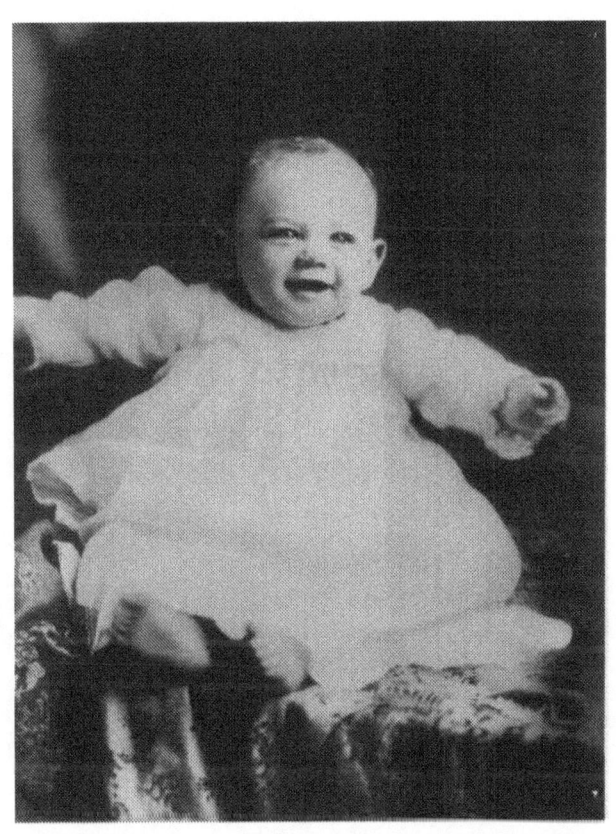

In My Christening Dress

Ol' Curly Head

With My Kiddie Bike

Playing with Bill

Feeding the Chicks

With a Few of My Biddies

In My Teddy-Bear Suit

Big Man

Ruth and I Ready for Sunday School

Right Before My First Day in School

After the Measles in the Second Grade

Horace and I Ready for Action

The Day after High School Graduation

Mama and Daddy

WHAT ARE MOTHERS?

God could not be everywhere, and so he made mothers.—Jewish Proverb

Children are what their mothers are.—Walter Savage Landor

Men are what their mothers made them.—Ralph Waldo Emerson

All that I am my mother made me.—John Quincy Adams

All that I am, or hope to be, I owe to my angel mother.—Abraham Lincoln

Of all the rights of women, the greatest is to be a mother.—Lin Yutang

I think it must somewhere be written, that the virtues of mothers shall be visited on their children.—Charles Dickens

The future destiny of the child is always the work of his mother. Let France have good mothers, and she will have good sons—Napoleon Bonaparte

The future of society is in the hands of mothers.—de Beaufort

Mothers make men.—Thomas Jefferson

My mother was the making of me.—Thomas Edison

The mother in her office holds the key of the soul, and she it is who stamps the coin of character.—From an Old Play

It is at our mother's knee that we acquire our noblest and truest and highest ideals.—Mark Twain

A man never sees all that his mother has been to him till it's too late to let her know that he sees it.—William Dean Howells

A mother holds her children's hands for a while, their hearts forever.—Author Unknown

The mother's heart is the child's schoolroom.—Henry Ward Beecher

One good mother is worth a hundred schoolmasters.—George Herbert

All I am I owe to my mother. I attribute all my success in life to the moral, intellectual and physical education I received from her.—George Washington

No language can express the power and beauty and heroism and majesty of a mother's love.—E. H. Chapin

Love began with waking up and loving my mother's face.—George Eliot

What are Raphael's Madonnas but the shadow of a mother's love, fixed in permanent outline forever.—Thomas W. Higginson

An ounce of mother is worth a pound of clergy.—Spanish Proverb

A mother understands what a child does not say.—Proverb

The hand that rocks the cradle rules the world.—Proverb

POEMS THAT REMIND ME OF MAMA

The Watcher

She always learned to watch for us,
Anxious if we were late,
In winter by the window,
In summer by the gate.

And though we mocked her tenderly,
Who had such foolish care,
The long way home would seem more safe
Because she waited there.

Her thoughts were all so full of us,
She never could forget,
And so I think that where she is
She must be watching yet,

Waiting till we come home to her,
Anxious if we are late,
Watching from Heaven's window,
Leaning from Heaven's gate.

—Margaret Widdener

Don't Think Of Her As Gone Away

Don't think of her as gone away,
Her journey's just begun,
Life holds so many facets,
This earth is only one.

Just think of her as resting,
From sorrows and from tears,
Somewhere in warmth and comfort,
Where there're no days and years.

Think how she must be wishing,
That we could know today,
That nothing but our sadness,
Can really pass away.

Just think of her as living,
In hearts of those she touched,
For nothing loved is ever lost
And she is loved so much.

—Anonymous

ARE YOU A "TRUE EUFAULIAN"?

Only a true Eufaulian knows what "cattywompus" means.

Only a true Eufaulian knows the difference between a "hissie fit" and a "conniption fit." And they don't have them, they pitch them.

Only a true Eufaulian can show or point out to you the general direction of "yonder."

Only a true Eufaulian knows exactly how long a time "directly" is, as in "I'm going to town. Be back directly."

Even true Eufaula babies know that "Gimme some sugar" is not asking for the white, granular sweet substance that sits in a pretty little round bowl in the middle of the table.

All true Eufaulians know exactly when "by and by" is.

Only a true Eufaulian knows that the best way to show you care when a neighbor's got trouble is to carry the neighbor a plate of hot fried chicken and a big bowl of cold potato salad. If the neighbor's trouble is real bad, a big bowl of banana puddin' is added.

Only true Eufaulians grow up knowing the exact difference between "right near" and "a right far piece." They also know that "just down the road" can be 1 mile or 20.

A true Eufaulian knows that "fixin'" can be used as a noun, a verb, or an adverb.

Only a true Eufaulian knows that the word "booger" can be a resident of the nose, a description of a person as in "that ol' booger," or something scary that jumps out at you in the dark.

Only true Eufaulians make friends while standing in lines. And when they are in lines, they talk to everybody.

Put 100 true Eufaulians in a room and half of them will find out they're kin, even if only by marriage.

True Eufaulians know grits from cream of wheat and how to eat them.

Every true Eufaulian knows that tomatoes, green or ripe, fried in bacon grease are good with breakfast.

When you hear someone say, "I caught myself lookin'" at someone or something, you know you are in the presence of a true Eufaulian.

You are a true Eufaulian when you ask for "sweet tea" when you want your tea sweetened with lots of sugar, and "sweet milk" when you don't want buttermilk.

True Eufaulians call white bread "light bread" to distinguish it from dark bread or cornbread.

A true Eufaula boy who asks a girl if he can carry her to a dance doesn't mean he wants to tote her, he just wants to take her.

And if you are a true Eufaulian, you don't yell obscenities at little old ladies driving 10 MPH on Broad Street downtown. You just say to yourself, "Bless her heart," and slow down behind her.

MY POEMS

We look before and after,
And pine for what is not.
Our sincerest laughter
With some pain is fraught.
Our sweetest songs are those that tell of saddest thought.
—From "To a Skylark," by Percy Bysshe Shelley

WALKING TOGETHER

You are with me
In my every dream,
Walking together
In love, as a team.

Life surely blessed me
By giving me you,
I never dreamed that
Such dreams could come true.

But still here you are
Right by my side,
Holding my hand
With our every stride

Walking through life
With a love so true,
And I am so happy
To walk it with you.

So across the years
I'll walk with you,
In forests green,
On shores of sand.

And when our time
On earth is through,
In heaven, too
You'll have my hand.

Thank you, darling, for walking with me.
It's been a wonderful journey!

TO KAY, WITH LOVE

Here's to Kay, the love of my life,
A wonderful mother, a wonderful wife,
To years of joy, full free of strife,
With rampant love and happiness rife
To sun-filled days, to walks on the beach,
Hand in hand, or at arm's reach.
I think that I shall never see,
A poem lovely, Kay, as thee.

My toast to Kay at her 70th birthday brunch at the Cypress, October 15, 1995:
"To this wonderful lady, who has shared her life and love with me for many
years, who has blessed me with two fine boys and four fine grandchildren, and
in so many other ways." Then I read my poem.

THIS FLOWER

How can I kiss you when you're gone?
How can I hold you when day's done?
How can I love you each long hour?
I can't.
But I can kiss…
And hold…
And love…
This flower you left behind.

TRUTH

Truth
Is
Like a small piece of sculpture
Carved from a large piece of granite.
The truth-seeker
Chips away at the granite,
Hewing away huge chunks of useless rock,
Until
What is left
Is
Truth.

HEARTQUAKES

I cried when you left me last night.
Deep agony welled from my heart,
Like rumblings of an earthquake.
First faint, then loud, then thundering,
As if the earth itself were shaken
              by some unknown force....
Some deep-hidden, rolling, body-shaking,
              bone-breaking, jaw-breaking force.
I felt my very being break in pieces,
Just like a fragile leaf in swirling waters.
And after the agony came the rain—Niobe-like,
              deep-welling from the heart,
Bursting its way through my eyes,
Pouring down my cheeks,
Dropping on the shaking ground.
Then I cried:
"Oh, God! What can I do? Help me! Please!"
Then, like distant thunder, the heartquake
              gradually died away.
The rumbling stopped. The shaking ceased.
The rain dwindled to tiny droplets.
The agony had gone from my heart....
I know that deep in my heart agony still lives,
Waiting to well again, to thunder again,

to shake my very being,
To make the path for the rain to follow.
And I know this will happen when I least expect:
A poem read…a song heard…a sunset seen…
Or just a stray thought, to start the welling again….
How many years will agony dwell in my heart?
When will these heartquakes cease?
I look for many more…for may more…for many more.
I do not know what heartquakes measure on love's Richter scale,
But oh, I know the wreckage that they leave behind them…
In my heart, from whence they came.

I"LL REMEMBER YOU

In the rising of the sun and the setting of the moon…
        I'll remember you.
In the blowing of the summer wind and in the winter's chill…
        I'll remember you.
In the blossoming of buds and the birth again of spring…
        I'll remember you.
In the blueness of the sky and the blackness of the night…
        I'll remember you.
In the rustling of the leaves and the brown of autumn sheaves…
        I'll remember you.
At the start of every year and the ending with a tear…
        I'll remember you.
When I have joys to share and griefs alone to bear…
        I'll remember you.
So long as I may live you too shall live,
For now you are a part of me, and…
        I'll remember you.

I'D LIKE

I'd like the memory of me
        To be a happy one,
I'd like to leave an afterglow
        Of smiles when life is done.

I'd like to leave an echo
　　　　Whisp'ring softly down the ways,
Of happy times and laughing times
　　　　And bright and sunny days.

I'd like the tears of those who grieve
　　　　To dry before the sun
Of happy memories I leave…
　　　　When all my life is done.

ABOUT THE AUTHOR

Dozier Copeland Cade was born in 1917 in Eufaula, Alabama, and was graduated from high school there. He holds bachelor, master and doctor's degrees from the University of Alabama, Northwestern University and the University of Iowa, respectively. He was a newspaperman about 10 years, working in reporting and editing assignments on the Eufaula (Ala.) Tribune, the Tuscaloosa (Ala.) News, the Atlanta Journal, and the Chicago Daily News. For 30 years he was a Journalism teacher and administrator at Emory University, Northwestern University, Georgia State University and the University of Tennessee, where he was Director of the School of Journalism. He also was a Public Relations practitioner and consultant, and worked for a while as a Journalism textbook consultant and reader for the Macmillan Company. During World War II he served with the Office of Strategic Services in China, where he received the Special Breast Order of the Cloud and Banner from the Chinese government, and retired from the military with the rank of Colonel after 30 years of Active and Reserve service in the Army. He and his wife Catherine Woodman (Kay) Cade live on Hilton Head Island, S.C. in the Cypress, a retirement community. They have two sons, Dr. James Ellis Cade of New Orleans and Dozier Woodman Cade of Nashville. Dozier's sister, Ruth Cade White, lives in Eufaula. This is his first published book.

0-595-30741-8